Great Plains Patchwork

Great Plains Patchwork

A MEMOIR

MARILYN COFFEY

Iowa State University Press / Ames

FRONTISPIECE: *My great grandfather's farmstead, Cassbrook, on the banks of Nebraska's Sappa Creek. James Coffey purchased it in 1885.*

"Plainsong" first appeared, under the title "In Praise of Plains," in *Natural History* (November 1981). "The Dust Storms" first appeared in *Natural History* (February 1978). "The Great Lincoln Bank Robbery" first appeared in *Magazine of the Midlands* (January 29, 1989). "My Flood Story" first appeared in the Hastings (Nebr.) *Daily Tribune* (June 1, 1985) and the Clay Center (Kans.) *Dispatch* (June 1, 1985); it is based on an interview conducted by the author with Arlene Dake Mintzmyer, and is reprinted with the permission of Arlene Dake Mintzmyer. "Badlands Revisited" first appeared in *Atlantic Monthly* (December 1974), and is reprinted with the permission of *Atlantic Monthly*.

Manufactured in the United States of America

First edition, 1989

Library of Congress Cataloging-in-Publication Data

Coffey, Marilyn.
    Great Plains patchwork / Marilyn Coffey. — 1st ed.
        p. cm.
    ISBN 0–8138–0341–1
    1. Nebraska—Description and travel. 2. Nebraska—Social life and customs. 3. Great Plains—Description and travel. 4. Great Plains—Social life and customs. 5. Coffey, Marilyn—Childhood and youth.
I. Title.
F670.C63   1989
978—dc20   89–34091
                                               CIP

To Ted Solotaroff
who encouraged me to write about my homeland —
the Great Plains

to Carole Rosenthal
whose timely suggestion that I write about Badlands
started this book rolling

and to my family
past, present, and future —
both those bonded by blood and those bonded by earth

Contents

Acknowledgments

My debts abound. To try to name each person and organization who assisted, in large or small part, in the creation of *Great Plains Patchwork* would be a fool's errand. However, I do want to thank some whose help, encouragement, and support mean a lot to me. In particular:

The late Wilbur Gaffney, professor emeritus, University of Nebraska-Lincoln, once my creative writing teacher, who always seemed to stay at least one verbal step ahead of me and who suggested I investigate the Great Lincoln Bank Robbery.

Bev Meier, college roommate, one of my earliest and staunchest supporters.

Those writers whose works stimulated my curiosity about the Great Plains, particularly Mari Sandoz, but also Meridel LeSueur, Willa Cather, and Hamlin Garland.

Grant Wood, whose *American Gothic* taught me to notice the Great Plains' medieval aspect.

The varied and marvelous institutions of research that exist in this country, but particularly the New York Public Library's historical division (for its fine collection of early plains diaries), the Nebraska State Historical Society (for its excellent Great Plains research facilities, including photographs), and the Library of Congress.

The many archivists and librarians who, as part of their day's work, patiently helped me with my research, and particularly Marty Miller, Research Assistant for Photographs, Nebraska State Historical Society.

Arlene Dake Mintzmyer, who entrusted me with the task of listening to her painful story.

Those residents of Harlan County, Nebraska, who shared their memories of the Republican River flood of 1935.

My family, those modern-day purveyors of the Coffey myth, especially my father, our official and unofficial raconteur, whose *The Coffey Family History* and "My Private War with Hoffa" (*Saturday Evening Post*) were particularly helpful; my uncle Vic, for his assistance in preparing "The Coffey Boys" and "Hail"; my sister Margery, who dipped into her artwork for my title; my sister Margaret Dent, my aunts Mabel and Mary Coffey and Faith Kemper, for help with photographs, and my mother, for introducing me to the pleasures of the written word.

My many friends and colleagues at Pratt Institute, Brooklyn, New York, who have been supportive of my writing, and particularly President J. Richardson Pratt, Jr., a Nebraskan by adoption; Dean George Lowy and his competent staff of librarians, often the first to hear my research problems, especially Tad Kumatz, Margo Karp, and Jo McSweeney; Dean Jack Minkoff and the faculty of the School of Liberal Arts and Sciences, especially Carl Craycraft, Chair, Department of English and Humanities, Estelle Horowitz, Rosemary Palms, "Chick" Chickering, and my writing buddies: Jane Augustine, Rolf Fjelde, Kathleen Early Hopkins, Suzanne McConnell, Richard Perry, and Carole Rosenthal.

The network of writers and other artists who inspire me, teach me, and sustain me when the going gets rough, particularly Sheron Thompson for her reading of the manuscript, Linda Metcalf and Toby Simon for their long-term friendship, and Lynda Schor for her humor, as well as Harlene Allen, Donnette Atiyah, Nolan Baer, Vern and Ananda Barnet, Lian Brandon, Amy Ganz, Anita Feldman, Lorraine Inzalaco, Licio Isolani, Shirley Powell, Mickey Revenaugh, Robert Roth, Robert Sasse, Laura Sharpe, Shirley Smith, Joe Wetmore, Barbara Zanditon, Barbara Zapatka, and many others.

Brooklyn College where I studied creative writing, particularly my tutors, Jonathan Baumbach, Maureen Howard, Joan Larkin, and Peter Spielberg, as well as Les Von Losberg and my other classmates, who dissected several chapters for me.

Elaine Markson Literary Agency, for its verve in helping me market chapters, and especially to Elaine Markson and Geri Thoma.

The magazine and newspaper editors who published chapters from the book, particularly Carol Breslin at *Natural History* and Mike Curtis at *Atlantic Monthly*.

The staff at Iowa State University Press, whose enthusiasm for *Great Plains Patchwork* transformed to pleasures the many chores of taking a work from manuscript to a book in a store, and particularly to those I know best: Richard R. Kinney, Director; Bill Silag, Managing Editor; R. Dixon Smith, Manuscript Editor; and Hugh M. Schultz, Marketing Director.

All those persons I didn't mention by name but without whose assistance, encouragement, and support the creation of *Great Plains Patchwork* would have been decidedly more difficult and distinctly less pleasurable.

None of the people mentioned, of course, is answerable for one word in this book. That responsibility is mine alone.

MARILYN COFFEY

Great Plains Patchwork

Prologue: PLAINSONG

I drink the wind like wine.
— HAMLIN GARLAND

The Great Plains region of the United States, where I was born and raised, is part of an enormous strip of flatland that stretches alongside the Rocky Mountain chain for more than three thousand miles, from the plateaus of northern Mexico to the Mackenzie River in subarctic Canada. In sheer extent, this North American grassland has no equal on earth, although similar areas exist on other continents: the steppes of Siberia, the pampas of South America, the veldts of Africa. Shaped roughly like the crescent of the waxing moon, the Great Plains swells to its

The Platte River's flat water mirrors a spectacular sunset, a common occurrence on the Great Plains. Courtesy Nebraska State Historical Society.

maximum in central United States, tapers to near points at its termini. Once, not much more than a hundred years ago, this plain was nothing but meadow, a tangled profusion of grasses and wild flowers that was broken only by an occasional tree-lined river or stream meandering slowly downslope or by buffalo and Indian trails which crisscrossed each other in an intricate but delicate network that led from waterway to waterway.

As a child, my keenest pleasure was to ride unhindered, bareback on my Indian pony, across this great sweep of meadowland, a fantasy that required only the window seat of our family car as it sped down the straightaway that nearly every Great Plains road provides. The view through the windshield would not do; it was time-fixed. Through the windshield, one saw the Great Plains split in two by a ribbon of asphalt rimmed with roadside ditches and decorated with telegraph poles, stuck in the earth like candles in a cake, holding a wire which strung from coast to coast. But through the side window at sixty miles an hour, instead of a blur of neatly furrowed fields or monochrome squares of golden wheat bounded by barbed wire, I could see, by merely squinting my eyes, the prairie as it must have looked unfolding beneath Coronado's visor or over the bow of Father Marquette's birchbark canoe, its variegated grasses and blooms interwoven into a canvas of the richest tweed, subtle colors blending with one another, shifting under the welter of the wind, shaded by the play of clouds casting shadows from the sky. Here, content, I could ride alone for hours, my hair streaming behind me like my mustang's mane and tail, my left hand cupping the rein that stretched out like a rawhide nerve between me and my steed's velvet mouth, my right hand waving wild and free. On and on we would ride, on and on and on, flying as the car sped, due east or west, following those paths that once were ruts cut by wagon wheels that followed earlier paths pounded deep by the thundering hooves of countless buffalo, through what Shimek in 1911 called the "monotonous magnitude." Monotonous? Such a thought never occurred to me. It was the thought of an outsider, one who is passing through. A native would never think such a thing, not here, by the side window in the back seat, the tires singing in her ears, here where every moment of time and movement of self changed one's relationship to the infinite space, here where one intuitively knew how to watch the shifting of the wind as, later, one would be taught to watch one's meditating breath, here where the earliest lesson learned from the land was that beauty and subtlety were inexorably intertwined.

I never actually laid eyes on virgin prairie when I was young. Except for scattered fragments of it, some of which can still be seen today, virtually all of the native grassland of the central plains had been plowed under long before I was born. In fact, my great-grandfathers James Thomas Coffey and Isaac Matts Smith were two of the hundreds of small farmers who resolutely overturned the sod, Smith in 1883 and Coffey in 1885, burying the last generation of native meadow deep in the Tertiary soil out of which its ancestors had sprung millions of years ago. But that didn't matter to me. I knew how the prairie must have been, not because I had been told, but because some vestige of it seemed to cling to me with the stubbornness of the afterlife of a recently amputated limb, as though knowledge of what the land had once been entered me through my very pores, carried, perhaps, by the ceaseless wind. It was, paradoxically, the most beautiful land I had ever seen.

Reports of the virgin prairie's beauty, written by early explorers and naturalists, confirm my childhood intuition. Journal entry after entry describes the vast meadows that were profusely decorated—gilded with myriad flowers. The fields of Quivara, in central Kansas, were "covered with flowers of a thousand different kinds, so thick that they choked the pasture," wrote the Spanish explorer Onate in 1601. "A thousand young flowers gemmed the grassy plains," wrote Thomas J. Farnham some two hundred years later. There were the sky-blue flowers of spiderwort and the light red phlox, the showy yellow sunflowers and purple asters, fields full of white flowers and long garlands of wild roses whose single corolla of pale pink petals surrounded a chunky golden stamen and whose fragrance lay heavy in the early spring air. "These vast plains, beautiful almost as the fancied Elysium, were enamelled with innumerable flowers," wrote English botanist Thomas Nuttall in 1819, "an uncommon variety of flowers of vivid tints, possessing all the brilliancy of tropical productions."

As profuse and varied as the flowers, although less spectacular, were the grasses which ranged in height from the short stubby buffalo and gramma grasses of the semiarid western prairie through the thick luxuriant mixed grasses of the subhumid central prairie, about ten inches high, to the great swaying blades of bluestem and Indian grass in the humid eastern prairie, blades that rose eight feet high. These heights were directly proportional to the rainfall, which tapers off from east to west, as can be seen today by the commercial grasses that have replaced the native strains. In the east, our corn, a grass, rustles higher than a man's head, while the less humid central region is renowned for another, shorter, grass: winter wheat. The semiarid western prairie, then as now, was good primarily for grazing, its clumps of short grass mixing with the prickly pear and with the sunflower, a tiny wild flower in the west, taller than a tulip in the central plains, and eight feet high in the east. The central plains, where I grew up, was a transitional area, dependent on the intermittent rain, which never seemed to fall twice in the same place. In dry years, needlegrass and other short grasses from the west would intrude to mix with the central prairie's June grass and wheat grass at the top of sunbaked ravines; in wetter years, big and little bluestem would creep in from the east, taking hold along moisture-laden ravine bottoms.

This stunning panorama of wild flowers and native grasses, their species described meticulously by early botanists, would probably strike the modern eye as one vast, impressionistic canvas swept by variegated colors that changed with the prairie's varied moods. How delicate this meadow must have appeared in the blue light of an early morning, as bland morning breezes bent the tips of grasses, displaying the muted colors of the blades' undersides. How vivid at midday, the sky as clear as in a Chinese painting, when through the crystal light, according to artist Thomas Mails, you could see a spot of color twenty miles away. Or after a shower when the grass was "gemmed with the reflection of innumerable pendant raindrops," according to Major Stephen Harriman Long. And how serene under the purple light of a quiescent evening, when deer might be seen stepping through the shoals which separated sand bars on a meandering river like the Platte—a "stilly scene, like shadows of phantasmagoria, or Ossian's deer made of mist," wrote Henry Marie Brackenridge.

Not only did colors shift with the various moods of each prairie day but also with each season: white in winter, green in spring, yellow in summer, and red-orange in autumn, says Mails, but that simplifies the matter too much in a land where winter may look like a mirror as a sudden drenching of February rain turns the plains into a continuous sheet of water. Or brown, as snow melts to reveal the stubborn remnants of the prairie grass, some of which live for twenty years. In early spring, the slender shoots of bright new grass may well sprout up a sharp and tender green in the winter-yellowed sward. But spring, like autumn, is when the wild flowers reach their peak of intensity, glazing the meadow with purples, pinks, red, yellow, and white. In the overplus of August's brittle light, sere stubble may suddenly mirage into an islanded lake, while through the October haze of a reddened Indian summer sun, the prairie colors are seen as though wrapped in smoke.

The beauty of the Great Plains, however, is not for everyone. The space I took for granted as a child—what the Plains Indians called the Waho, the great circle, the circle of the horizon—was more than most newcomers, whose ideas of space had been formed in hilly, tree-studded country, could bear. "The first experience of the plains, like the first sail with a 'cap' full of wind, is apt to be sickening," wrote an early viewer, Colonel Dodge. More than one traveler, in diary or letter, told of standing still and lonely, overwhelmed by the silence and vastness of the place. "Magnificent, though melancholy," wrote Henry Brackenridge in 1811, while Thomas Farnham noted, in 1839, that his eyes ached from his attempts to embrace the view. Many a writer mentioned a general feeling of emptiness or dwelt on the nauseating loneliness. Even Coronado, who must have been reminded of portions of his native Spain when he entered this dry, treeless land, expressed surprise at its scope, saying, "I came upon some plains so vast that in my travels I did not reach their end, although I marched over them for more than three hundred leagues"—nearly one thousand miles, as we measure land.

The plains were most frequently compared, by early journal writers, to an ocean, an ocean where one swell melted imperceptibly into another. Some, like expedition leader Wilson P. Hunt, used this figure of speech literally. "The limits of the visible horizon," wrote Hunt, "are as exactly defined, and the view as extensive as at sea, the undulations on the surface of the earth here bearing no greater proportion in scale than the waves of an agitated ocean." Others were more poetic. Thomas Farnham called the plains "vast savannahs, resembling molten seas of emerald sparkling with flowers, arrested while stormy and heaving, and fixed in eternal repose." Adopting a more tragic perspective Abbé Emmanuel H. Domenech wrote, in 1860, that the grasslands of west Texas were "like an ocean of dark stunted herbs, in which not a single bush or bramble obstructed the view, where nothing marked a beginning or an end, and where all was mute and motionless." Some, like the young American scientist Brackenridge, found the ocean comparison inadequate. "If the vast expanse of the ocean is considered a sublime spectacle," he wrote of the central plains in 1811, "this is even more so; for the eye has still greater scope." Or, as Hamlin Garland would put it decades later, "my eyes/Fasten on more of earth and air/ Than sea-shores furnish anywhere."

Those to whom the vast open space was not oppressive found it, as I did, exhilarating. "The nerves stiffen, the senses expand, and man begins to realize the magnificence of being," wrote Colonel Dodge, once he'd recovered from his seasickness. Brackenridge, who had stepped out onto the plains from a Missouri river boat, wrote: "Instead of being closed up in a moving prison, deprived of the use of our limbs, here we may wander at will. The mind naturally expands, or contracts, to suit the sphere in which it exists—in the immeasurable immensity of the scene, the intellectual faculties are endued with an energy, a vigor, a spring, not to be described."

Exhilaration, however, could tip quickly into terror, and often did, particularly when unprepared travelers first met the Great Plains' thunder bird, that spectacular mythological creature which flies through the air with its eyes closed, its gigantic wings flapping out "peals of thunder which seemed to shake the earth to its centre," thunder which visibly enraged the buffalo bulls who pawed the earth and bellowed as the big bird rumbled overhead. When the thunder bird blinked, the Indians said, great spears of sprangling lightning would flash out of its open eyes, leaving the pack animals to huddle abjectly together, heads drooping and limbs stilled, while humans trembled for their lives.

The Great Plains is justifiably famous for its violent thunderstorms, one of the more dramatic aspects of the region's changeable, highly versatile weather. The storms, typically of short duration, often produce downpours of three to six inches or more. The rain tends to be local, drenching the earth in one spot while the surrounding area remains dry. Most thunderstorms are caused when two of the region's three major air masses collide, when the cold dry air from Canada strikes either warm moisture-laden air masses from the Gulf of Mexico or air that has swept across the Rocky Mountains, Pacific air masses which range from warm to cold, moist to dry. Most rain falls from April to July, with storms reaching their maximum in May or June, the months when most early travelers began their long treks into, or across, the plains. As a result, early journals abound with tales of travelers drenched to their skins, spending cold, sleepless, wet nights, unable to find a bit of dry bedding or clothing among all their gear. Along the Platte River, famous for drawing thunderstorms, emigrants reported almost daily downpours in the spring of 1839.

Anyone who has seen a Great Plains thunderstorm in its full splendor knows that its most spectacular feature, the thing that distinguishes it most clearly from an equally violent downpour in the city, is the simple fact that the storm can be seen coming from miles away. Indeed, the plains area is so large that a storm, from a distance, can be perceived as a single entity, its black clouds churning, its lightning jets leaping, its gray sheet of rain falling in a slant torrent even while the sun shines directly overhead. Before the storm is seen, it can be heard, its thunder rumbling gently from a great distance. And before it can be heard, it can be felt: a shift in the temperature of the air, a certain silencing of the wind. "Excepting the sound of distant thunder, which was continual," wrote John Bradbury, English naturalist, of a prairie storm in May, 1810, "an awful silence prevailed, and the cloud which had already spread over one half of the visible horizon was fast shutting out the little remains of daylight." As the cloud drew overhead, he noted that it was of "a pitchy blackness, and so dense as to resemble a solid body, out of which, at short intervals, the lightning poured in a continual stream for one or two seconds. Darkness came on with a rapidity I never before witnessed." He wrapped himself in a blanket and lay down on the open land. "The lightning," wrote Farnham of a storm in 1839, "was intensely vivid," as three black clouds, one in the southeast, one in the southwest, and one in the northeast, "rose with an awful rapidity towards the zenith." As he looked up, he saw the cloud "rent in fragments, by the most terrific explosion of electricity we had ever witnessed." Peal upon peal of thunder followed, as burning bolts leapt from cloud to cloud, enveloping the land in a "lurid glare."

Hail often accompanied these storms, although the size of hailstones seems curiously to diminish with the passing of time. One of Coronado's conquistadors, Pedro de Castañeda of Náxera, reported hail in the southern plains in 1541 "as large as bowls and even larger, and as thick as raindrops, that in places they covered the ground to the depth of two and three and even more spans." The huge stones destroyed their tents, dented their armor, bruised their horses, and broke all their pottery, a problem for the Spanish army since the local Indians, who ate only fruit and meat, had no use for crockery and could supply them with none. Many years later on the plains, a report circulated of an Indian who had been knocked down by a hailstone the size of a goose egg. As for myself, although I stood on our screened-in back porch through many a summer storm with my father, a farm boy who never tired of watching it rain, and although I saw countless white stones fall from the sky and bounce across our green lawn, I cannot say that I ever saw a prairie hailstone larger than a marble, although some were as big as taws. However, the folks over at Republican City swore they'd seen hail the size of ping-pong balls, and they had cars with bashed-in windshields to prove it.

These violent thunderstorms stunned the senses of those who lived through them, protecting themselves as best they could against the elements. Some, of course, were killed. After an unexpected storm in the spring of 1855, a caravan of emigrants found that its four guards had been knocked down and that another man lay insensible in his tent. "A Mr. Myers," wrote Lydia Waters, one of the caravan, "who had a nice carriage, got into it to keep the blinds down to prevent the lining from getting wet, and was found sitting in the front seat dead. The lightning had struck the top of his head and run down his neck and side, escaping out of the carriage without leaving a mark, except for a very small bit of broken moulding on the top." Early the next morning, the travelers gave Mr. Myers a typical prairie burial. "He was dressed in his best clothes, wrapped first in a sheet and then in a patchwork quilt. The men dug a deep grave and cut cottonwood and laid it over him to quite a thickness to prevent the coyotes from unearthing his body—which no doubt they did anyway. We had seen numbers of graves destroyed that way." Waters kept a lock of Mr. Myers' hair, burnt off by the lightning, to give to his wife, who'd been left with a three-months-old child. "No one else had thought of cutting it for her," she wrote.

Less dramatic than the storms, but equally unnerving—at least for some— was the prairie's *trompe l'oeil*. Optical illusions, caused by the combination of a rarified, transparent atmosphere with distances so great that "only the curvature of the earth's surface limits the view," often fooled the eye of the inexperienced observer. Objects, which could be seen with remarkable clarity from a great distance, became strangely distorted. Some were magnified, so that a raven might be mistaken for an Indian or an antelope for the much larger elk. Some were diminished, so that the leafy tops of a line of timber along a distant river seemed to "wave and mingle among the grass of the wild swelling meadows." Some, objects like tufts of grass or buffalo bones, were elevated, stretching up so high that they looked like humans. The first to mention this phenomenon was one of Coronado's chroniclers, who wrote that the land where buffalo roamed was "so level and bare that whenever one looked at them, one could see the sky between their legs, so that at a distance they looked like trimmed pine tree trunks with foliage joining at the top." Sometimes, under the intense glare of a pitiless August sun, the "earth and sky seemed to blend." In its most extreme form, this illusion became a mirage, such as the one described in 1849 by Alonzo Delano: "The glare of the sun upon the distant plain resembled the waves of a sea, and there were appearances of islands and groves."

This "abnormal land" was home to me. As I was growing up, I knew no other world but the prairie's vast Waho, its thunderstorms, its wind-blown fields. This natural habitat would render agoraphobia—the fear of open spaces—as incomprehensible to me as, many years later, my claustrophobia when ringed in by mountains or trees would confuse those who judged such restrictions "natural." Like a medieval woman, I was limited by the world I knew but knew not that my world was limited. What was "abnormal" to historian Walter Webb, whose book *The Great Plains* is justly considered a classic in this field, became gradually my norm. As a result, history—after a generation or two—became increasingly a dichotomy for me, as I suspect it must for anyone who has grown up in this magnificent region. With whom, at last, does one identify? For isn't history, in the final analysis, a question of deciding who one's ancestors are? Here the dichotomy began. Which did I value more, the bond of body or the bond of earth? The enigma became a question of heredity versus environment. I was, of course, an American. But who were my people? Were they the Europeans—the

Scotch, Irish, English, and Germans with whom I claimed a common gene? Or were they the Pawnee, those stargazers who, for nearly five hundred years, had hunted across the acres that my great-grandparents farmed, whose paths, worn thin by trailing tipi poles, became our roads, whose villages like ours, dotted the bluffs along the local rivers, the Republican, the Loup, and the Platte. To identify with the Europeans meant to lay claim to an intellectual ancestry that went back to classical Greece. But to identify with the Pawnee, to embrace land as the more lasting bond, was to lay ahold of another kind of history altogether, a history that preceded antiquity, a history some sixty-three million years old.

Bonded by blood: my father and mother, Tom and Zelma Coffey, in their Gay Twenties courtin' days.

Bonded by earth: the Pawnee Indians, those stargazers, lived along the Republican River long before my white ancestors put down roots there. Standing in center is 105-year-old Ruling-His-Son. Courtesy Nebraska State Historical Society.

PART I

Earth

The Coffey Boys

JAMES

I was born a second-generation Nebraskan on both my parents' sides. Like my mother and father, I knew no other home but what was contained in Harlan County and its environs, a world bordered on the north by the Platte River, on the south by Kansas, and on the east and west by the sun.

To grow up in the middle of the United States this way gives one a different perspective on history than the typical Easterner has, an inside-out view, history viewed from deep within what would become the physical center of the United States. To one

The scruffy Coffey Boys, lined up on the running board by age (from left): Lyle, Vic, Paul ("Pat"), Ray, June ("Tom," my dad). Glen was not yet born.

born on the plains, early American history seems but a speck on the eastern horizon, something happening between England and the colonies that had little or nothing to do, then, with us. Gradually the speck looms larger, expanding in size as the United States increases in population until suddenly we're being invaded by wave after wave of Easterners: trappers, fur traders, explorers, caravans of white people headed toward Oregon, the railroad, the cavalry. All hell starts popping loose.

At this dramatic moment my family history seems, to me, to begin. Like a speck on the eastern horizon appears a wagon loaded with Coffeys. Driving is my great-grandfather James. He is forty-five years old and already sporting a beard that a later picture of him shows to be full and white. James has a squarish sort of face, rectangular, actually, with bushy brows and a smile that seems to play just beneath the surface of his skin. In the wagon with him is my round-faced great-grandmother Mary, from whom I've inherited my fine, perfectly flat, straight hair. She parted hers in the middle and wore it pulled back, almost skin tight, in what was probably a bun. With Mary are a bunch of kids: the Coffey brothers—Jim, Charley, Jack, Sam, Bill, Ben, and Art—and their sister Mary Ellen, then known as Nellie. My grandpa, the next to the youngest, is only three; Jim, the oldest, is sixteen. In my mind's eye, the Coffey wagon is bursting with offspring; at least one of them sits in the back, his legs dangling over the tailgate, his body jouncing with every turn of the heavy wooden wheels. I say they arrived in a wagon, although for all I know they may have arrived—as all the rest of my relatives did—by train. The year was 1885 and, at that time, people were traveling by both modes: my great-grandpa James was not part of the first wave of immigration into the central plains, but part of the second wave, the wave that came after the railroad was built.

All that happened to James prior to his arrival on the Great Plains—although recorded as part of our family history—seems vague to me since it happened, as it were, in a foreign country: Illinois. James had lived in Illinois for about twenty years, having married an Ohio woman, Mary E. Rhoades, there, and sired nine of what would be his ten children. One, Frank Milton, he buried there. James was a farmer near Bloomington, Illinois, for most of those twenty years. What else was there for someone of lower-class Irish origins to do but dig in the dirt or become cannon fodder? He'd already tried the latter, having served for three years in the volunteer infantry of Illinois, fighting for the north in the Civil War. The company he was with—Company C of the Thirty-third Illinois—saw action up and down the Mississippi River, from St. Louis to New Orleans, and James must have served well for he earned a corporal's rating within four months. But the most cursed campaign of the war, which involved a trip from New Orleans to Brazos, Texas, on a sea-going steamer, the *Clinton*, seems to have done him in. According to company memoirs, the men were packed on the upper deck with scarcely room to move, while their horses, wagons, and supplies swamped the lower deck. The *Clinton* hit rough weather. Seasickness was rampant, equipment was damaged, and the horses were pretty much "stoved up" and ruined. Enough was enough for James. He transferred out of the Thirty-third to the Ninety-ninth Illinois, losing his corporal's rank in the process.

James's life prior to Illinois is even more mysterious to me. He spent his early years in New York, working for a dairy farmer in return for his keep. He was only eleven when that began; I presume it was not a bad job for an orphan who, only a year earlier, had arrived off the boat from Ireland. As he grew older, he was paid for his work: a suit of clothes was his first year's wages. Still, this must have seemed better than the famine he and his siblings had faced in the county of Galway, Ireland, when he was still a boy. But as soon as he appears on the eastern horizon of the land I also knew to be my own, James becomes real to me. I can see him kidding his seven sons, his daughter Nellie, and his wife as they jounce along the wagon wheel—rutted road. I can imagine him swapping tales with other caravaners as they relax a little at the end of a long day's run, for James's ability to spin a tale was legendary, his legacy from Galway that he passed on down the family line. In Galway, James had been known as James O'Cobhthaigh, possessor of an ancient name that linked him to a druidic heritage; although anglicized to "Coffey," Cobhthaigh had no relationship to that dark, caffeinic liquid brewed each morning on the campfire before the caravaners set out. Instead, it was the name of a three-handled, leather drinking mug, a container so old that it was once part of a druidic ritual, an emblem of the ancient goddess, a container so stabilized in size and shape that for a time it served Ireland as a standard of measure. I expect that James spun a tale the way most Coffeys still do today—with a straight face and a highly developed sense of exaggeration. Not lying, exactly. Just stretching the truth. Only one of his jokes has come down to us, a joke perhaps developed on the wagon trail but certainly perfected in the local country store after his last child, George Marion, had been born on January 7, 1887. All the tale required was a gullible out-of-towner, say a salesman passing through, and a straight man to set James up, something the local storekeeper was only too happy to do. "Well, sir," the shopkeeper would tell the salesman, "this may be a small town, but we sure do grow some big families out here. Take Mr. Coffey, for instance," and he would gesture towards my great-grandpa, whereupon the drummer could be counted on to say, "Oh, is that right, Mr. Coffey? How many kids you got?"

"Eight boys," James would reply with a straight face, "and every one of them has a sister."

I can imagine the smile flickering under his skin as he watched the salesman view him as the father of sixteen, rather than nine, and although I don't suppose he ever directly lied about the matter, I imagine he did carry on the joke as long as he could by whatever means came to mind. Should the out-of-towner blurt out, "Sixteen?" I don't expect that great-grandpa confessed it or denied it, but instead probably said something like, "Add 'em up!" Should his wife, Mary, have chided him, "Now James, you shouldn't have let that man think we had sixteen children," I expect that he would have replied what generations of Coffeys have said when backed into similar corners: "What he don't know won't hurt him."

This was the man that broke the sod out along Sappa

Creek, three miles southwest of Stamford, on land that would become known as the Coffey homestead but at that time was known as Cassbrook. He turned over soil that had lain unturned since the beginning of the Cenozoic era, some sixty-five million years ago, leaving marks in the earth's surface that will be visible to the trained eye millions of years hence, for the earth has a way of recording its own history and plow marks are known to last for millenniums. He must have been a man whose orientation was toward the future, not the past, for had he understood the past he would have, it seems to me, trembled before the enormity of what he was doing, altering the very elements of the earth. As the Cenozoic era began, the land mass that is North America had been formed; dinosaurs and flying reptiles were already extinct. The Rocky Mountains had risen, not once but twice, and the slopes of those rugged alps were furnishing detritus to the streams that flowed eastward over the plains, fanning out their deposits of sediment. The widespread seas that had once covered the area, when the oceans were at their largest, had receded, as though a quarrel between land and sea had finally been won by the land. But the flat ocean-like configuration remained. The Cassbrook farm must not have been much to look at, particularly to a farmer from Illinois: flat and dry, except down by the creek. The main building, a log house, had a slot in the door for people to drop their mail into should the family not be at home, for Cassbrook was the local post office in those days. Another building, a monstrosity, sat on the land. It had been built from native cottonwood when the lumber was still green and, as the wood aged, had become so twisted and warped that it was no longer usable for a building. Yet here James managed to carve out a homestead for himself and his family, sufficient to support his eight boys, each of whom had a sister, his daughter, and his wife.

No one can live forever. Mary was the first to go. In 1891, when she was about forty-six years old, a creeping paralysis set in that four years later, in the spring of 1895, would claim her life. The household shuddered and reorganized itself around Nellie, by this time eighteen and ready to shoulder her mother's responsibilities. She remained half-sister, half-mother to the Coffey brothers for the rest of her life, never marrying but moving from household to household as the brothers set up farmsteads of their own, to help with birthing and baking as the family needed her. She had a rough and rowdy sense of humor, like the boys. I remember her still, a robust old lady with Mary's round head and flat hair, confined to her wheelchair but seeming larger than life to the kid I was then, pounding her cane on the ground and barking if she wanted anything. She was the most ferocious lady I'd ever met, with a loud gravelly voice and a wart with a hair growing out of it, but her desires were instantly catered to, partial payment for the work of her life.

James lived until 1909. His was an unusual death, although perhaps not for his time. He bought a pair of socks from a traveling salesman, as was common in those days, and subsequently wore a blister on his heel. He was poisoned by the dye in the sock; he contracted erysipelas, a streptococcus infection which inflamed his skin a deep red beneath his stark white beard and stilled his flickering smile forever.

THE COFFEY BROTHERS

My grandpa Ben was thirteen when his mother died and Nellie took over the household. He became Nell's helper in the kitchen. One day, when the brothers were busy stacking alfalfa in a field north of the house, Ben was sent out to call them in to dinner. The brothers must have taken exception to the tone of his voice, because the first thing Ben knew, Jack, who was twenty-one then, and Sam, seventeen, had caught him and tied him to the teeth of an over-shot hay stacker, pulled the stacker up in the air, secured it, and left Ben to meditate on the evil of his ways — or the disadvantage of his small size — while the rest of the brothers hightailed it to the house for the noon meal. This was a typical Coffey joke: rough, rowdy, and physical. Small wonder that boxing gloves were kept in the house for settling disputes. "Tap lightly" was the promise, but Ben had seen the way the fights would flare up. Only a few days earlier, when Jack and Sam had been going at it, one hard tap called for a harder tap until boxing gloves weren't enough and the fighters, their Irish blood boiling, began to call out for bare knuckles and a fight to the finish. If only Ben were bigger, he could take on Sam . . . but dinner lasted long enough to give Ben plenty of time to figure out how to get even. That afternoon he collected a matchbox full of yellow-jacket wasps, and he kept them in the box until they were in an evil humor. After Jack and Sam had gone to bed that night and were sound asleep, Ben slipped the matchbox beneath the covers, right between the two brothers, and opened it. His revenge was sweet: Jack and Sam were badly stung, so badly that it hardly mattered to Ben that he had to sleep with his door locked for the next couple of months.

This was the world that my grandpa Ben grew up in, he and his seven brothers. A rowdy world, likely to explode into a flurry of fists or curses but just as likely to explode into mirth. Nothing was valued more than a good joke, no matter what its price, and perhaps it's not surprising that, while Cassbrook stands no longer, the jokes remain.

There is the classic tale of Sam, who lost his foot when he was five years old. He had been playing in the granary, riding a saddle that was precariously balanced on a partition. When he fell off, he landed on the upturned blade of a sharp scythe that cut his foot off just in front of the ankle joint. Instead of an artificial foot, Sam wore a regular shoe with the front of it stuffed. This gave him his opportunity. One day at school he caught one of the girls watching him, so he reached down, took ahold of the toe of his shoe, and turned it around and around. The girl—or so the story goes—fainted.

There's the story of George and Art, the two youngest brothers, deciding to break a calf to drive. They rigged up a harness of some sort and hooked the calf up to the slop barrel for a cart. George got in to ride, while Art led the calf. All went well until the calf noticed the slop barrel following it, jerked away from Art, and ran off, dragging George and the overturned slop barrel behind him. They drove quite a distance before the harness broke, allowing George to pick himself up and see to his cuts and bruises.

There's the story of Jim and Charley, the two older brothers, riding an old two-wheeled cultivator. They would pull it to the top of a hill, then coast down with Jim — the oldest and the fleetest — holding up the tongue. Jim, understandably, soon tired of this game, but Charley insisted, and down the hill they sped as fast as Jim could run. At the bottom of the hill was a tree, and Jim rammed the end of the cultivator tongue square into the tree, bringing the cultivator to a sudden halt and catapulting Charley through the air.

And then there's the story of Charley and the pig. My father recorded it this way in *The Coffey Family History*: "On the old Coffey farm in early days was about the only ice-house in the country. The whole family of boys (married and at home) would fill it every winter for the sole purpose of having ice-cream on Sunday afternoon through the summer at their gatherings and scarcely a Sunday went by but some or all of the family were there to enjoy the treat.

"This particular year they had to go almost to Orleans to find enough water and ice to fill the house. While at their father's on the previous Sunday making plans for the fill, as it took several teams and wagons and lunch for horses and humans as well, Charley said to Jack and Sam: 'Now with you fellows batching, it won't be necessary for you to bring lunch. Renna will put up enough for you.'

"Sam grumbled, 'Oh, I suppose you think we can't cook.'

"So on the stated morning everyone started out early in the cold from their various homes to go to the appointed place to cut and load the ice.

"Charley, on the way down was walking beside his wagon to keep warm. And just why he picked up that little dead pig lying by the road side and tossed it on the hay in the wagon, he didn't know then, for he had no idea of using it in the manner he did.

"When he got to the designated place, several were there down over the river bank sawing ice, building a fire, etc. As he drove up he noticed Jack and Sam's wagon and sure enough there they had brought the forbidden lunch.

"A scheme soon took form in Charley's mind. Sure, why not play a joke on Sam. And since everyone was out of sight this was the logical time. Charley removed the lunch from the grape-basket and slipped in Mr. Piggy, who fit just to perfection. And with all the wrappings tucked smoothly back into place he went to join the ice harvesters.

"At noon Charley heated the coffee and spread out the lunch and called dinner. Sam came boastfully up the river bank and said, 'Did you get the lunch out of our wagon? I want to prove to you that bachelor fare isn't so bad.'

"Charley said 'No,' and reminded him he was told to forget it.

"Out Sam went after the basket and back he came to display his dinner contribution.

"Try to imagine his let-down feeling and shock when he uncovered the dead pig.

" 'Charley, you big fool,' he said and a good Coffey wrestle ensued. Sam and Charley rolled over and over in the snow, down the riverbank and almost into the hole cut in the ice. All this was accompanied with the side-splitting laughter of the group of brothers."

The Coffey brothers grew older, but they never outgrew the legacy of laughter that James had bequeathed to them. At a Coffey family reunion, one of the brothers, an old-timer by now, was seen to slip an ice cube down the pants of a young Coffey sprawled out on the grass. The youngster leaped up, all fists, and headed for his brother who hollered, "I didn't do it! I didn't do it!" and hid behind his elders while the brothers crowed. And Art, when he was about sixty-four and had lost his left leg because of bone cancer, used the occasion for joking. When asked, "How are you, Art?" his stock answer became, "I can't kick."

The Coffey boys — Ben's six sons — were just plain ornery. Take Tub, for instance. Tub's real name was Lyle; he was nicknamed for his girth. He had the Coffey weakness toward fat, but he excelled the other boys in that regard: he showed it first, while he was still a kid. Tub was the next-to-the-youngest Coffey boy; the youngest was Glen who, by all accounts, was the hothead of the family. Tub loved to tease him. He'd do nearly anything to get Glen's goat, but it wasn't necessary to do much. A few well-chosen words, perhaps about a girl, and Glen would be red in the face and swinging. Tub was three years older than Glen, old enough to take anything that Glen could dish out. His defense tactic was simple: he'd turn his back on Glen, double over, and let Glen pound away. When he got tired, he'd turn around, pick Glen up, carry him to the horse tank, and heave him in the water. Let him cool off a little. This teasing Glen all the way to the horse tank got to be a ritual, until one day Glen side-stepped Tub when Tub turned around to get him, broke free of his grab, and headed to the horse tank himself. When he got there, he jumped in. At least he'd had the satisfaction of not letting Tub heave him in.

Tub had an ornery streak in him, no doubt about that. One day when he was still in grade school, some one triggered him off. No one would say, afterwards, just what happened, and Tub never would tell. He wasn't much for talking, anyway. It was hard to imagine a Coffey who didn't talk at every opportunity, but Tub must have picked up on his quiet mother's side. He spoke little, and still does. Anyway, that day Tub turned into a wild bull. The first thing the family knew about it was when a neighbor boy rode into the Coffey farm on a horse. He found Vic, Tub's older brother by two years, at home. "Vic," he said, "you better get yourself over to the schoolhouse. Something's wrong. I don't know what it is, but Tub is mad. He's got kids on top of the schoolhouse, on top of the toilets, on top of the bell house. Tub's out in the middle of the ball diamond like a mad bull, and there ain't nobody around him, teacher or nobody else." Vic went over to the schoolhouse, and found that what the neighbor boy had said was true, but Tub was already cooling off by the time Vic got there.

Vic was ornery, too, but in a sneakier sort of way. One day, he and "Pat," his older brother by two years, were out shucking corn when, as Vic puts it, "Mother Nature called, and you know how it is; when she calls, you got to go." He was quite a ways ahead of Pat in the rows, so he squatted, and then he spotted this great big ear of corn over in Pat's row. He pulled the stalk over, grabbed the ear, and pulled the husks back on it. "Then I got down and done my business on it," he says. "Then I pulled the husks back over it and kind of stood it back up a little bit. I knew Pat wouldn't miss a great big ear, I knew he'd be sure and grab that. Well, and you know how you shuck corn," and Uncle Vic laughed one of his famous laughs, somewhere between a hoot and a holler. Pat grabbed the ear, all right. He let out a cuss that started Vic's team of horses running, so Vic jumped in his wagon, and Pat lit out after him. . . .

Pat's older brother was Ray, who always seemed like Vic's twin to me. And the oldest boy was my Daddy, who had been christened June. He was born June 12, and that was the excuse given for his name, but he maintained that his mother had wanted a girl and when she didn't get one, she gave her baby a girl's name, anyway. I feel sorry for Clara Coffey if a girl is what she had in mind, for from 1907 until 1919, a boy tumbled out every two or three years. Perhaps she wanted a daughter because she missed her sisters, Ursa and Grace, who lived back in McCook where she'd been raised, first in a dugout and later in a sod house. She must have adjusted to her rowdy ornery no-good brood of boys admirably, for Vic says of her, "She was always in with us for any fun that we wanted to have. But she was the quiet type. She always wanted to hold things down." Clara was raised in town, so everything on the farm was new to her. She liked farm life and rose to its challenges. She learned to be a crack shot and, or so my father swore, "She could cook chicken thirty-two different ways."

To be a Coffey was to be privileged. "I used to feel sorry for all the kids who weren't Coffeys," my father said. Not until I got to be an adult did I realize that this family of Coffey boys that my father was part of, and so clearly loved, was nothing but a bunch of dirt-poor, scruffy-haired, dirty-faced, bare-footed, ragged-pants kids, kids we wouldn't have deigned to look twice at if they'd shown up at school with us. My understanding of class was born.

Not surprisingly, I have an ambivalence about class: which was better, the smutty rowdy lower class out of which my father had sprung and to which a certain amount of earthiness clung, or the materialistic middle class which ate its steak smothered in mushrooms and had its kids' teeth straightened, the class into which my father had risen?

I was raised middle class myself, which meant that in addition to the attraction the lower class held for me, with its premium on humor and bluntness, it also generated a certain amount of fear. My father's family seemed to be so emotionally charged; its energy was so high and it seemed to have a certain indifference to harming the physical body. I remember Glen, youngest and handsomest of the Coffey boys, running his finger through the flame of a candle in a feat which, when I tried to emulate it, resulted in scorched flesh. This Glen found amusing. And there are stories of grandpa Ben falling head first from six to eight feet off the top of a header, landing on his head and shoulders and surviving. "He was badly shaken up and very stiff for a few days but never missed an hour's work in the harvest field," wrote my father. And the time Ben was struck in the shoulder and jaw with a six-pound sledge hammer: it knocked him down but not out. The Coffeys—both the brothers and the boys—seemed to have a kind of stamina that strikes me as awesome.

To be a Coffey was to be privileged at least in part because to be a Coffey was to be born Irish, and to be Irish was to be blessed with a rollicking sense of humor, for one thing, and with intelligence, for another. I never questioned this. I grew up assuming I was Irish, conveniently ignoring my mother's genetic input—Scotch, English, and German—as well as the genetic in-

The Coffey Boys, duded up in their formal best, pose in descending order of age: (top, left to right) June ("Tom," my father), Ray, Paul ("Pat"); (bottom, left to right) Vic, Lyle, Glen.

put of James's and Ben's wives. On St. Patrick's day we broke out the green, and Dad was known to have cut the tie off a man who failed to wear the color. We read Irish ghost stories that stood our hair on end, and sang Irish songs — not folk songs, but the Irish-American songs that my father played on our record-player: "With that same old shillelagh my father could lick a dozen" — or was it a hundred? — "men" is the line from one song. "Who threw the overalls in Mrs. Murphy's chowder?" is part of another's refrain. My allegiance to the old country was at least as strong as my allegiance to Nebraska, and certainly more colorful. I knew that James was one of thousands who fled the Emerald Isle because of the horrendous potato famine and, in my mind's eye, Ireland was closer to home than the East Coast.

But to be born a Coffey also meant to be born poor. Famine

was the specter that stalked my father's family. To starve to death was something that could conceivably happen to a person: James fled Ireland to escape just such a fate, grandpa Ben tussled — not altogether successfully — with the earth to avoid it. Ben was the biggest of the Coffey brothers. He stood six foot one in his stocking feet and weighed, at the end of his life, nearly 315 pounds. As a slimmer younger man he tipped the scales at 240 or 250. "He was all man," his son, Vic, says of him. "When he got ahold of the end of a log, it came." Ben was the best looking of the brothers, too, his features more regular, his thick black hair wavy, his generous mustache setting off the Irish handsomeness that he had inherited from his father, James. But he didn't have James's luck at farming. He was the poorest of the Coffey brothers, barely eking out an existence for himself, his wife Clara, and their six sons: June ("Tom"), Ray, Paul ("Pat"), Vic, Lyle ("Tub"), and Glen.

"We were so poor that we never ate an orange except at Christmas when we got one in the toe of our sock," said my father, to whom a fresh peach or a pink grapefruit from Texas was as much of a treat as anything a man could reasonably expect in a lifetime.

To be a Coffey was, at last, to have an overwhelming sense of family, of pride in family that was all out of proportion to the family's actual standing in the world.

Plagues of Grasshoppers

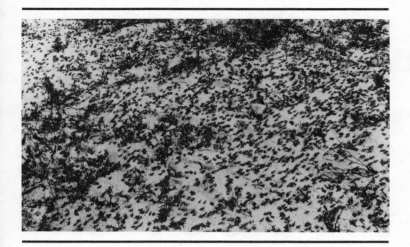

"A grasshopper sitting on a sweet 'tater vine, oh my, oh my." It was a line from one of my father's small repertoire of songs that he sang in the car when we headed north out of Nebraska, going to Minnesota to fish, an annual ritual for our family. I can see him singing yet, his big head with its slicked-back black hair thrown back, his voice quavering as it aimed at the right notes, and sometimes hit them, his style making up in energy what it lacked in precision. "Sing it again," my sisters and I would plead, and he'd comply. His was a jolly song that made the grasshopper seem a friendly creature, except for its tendency to "spit tobacco juice right in my eye." Sometimes in the heat of summer we'd catch the winged creatures with their V-shaped

A swarm of migrating, long-winged grasshoppers spreads like a blanket across a field, wings shimmering in the heat of the prairie sun, thousands of mouths voraciously feeding. Courtesy Nebraska State Historical Society.

legs, cup their quivering bodies in our hot hands until we could stand the movement no longer, then release them. The hoppers would sail off into the air like butterflies or moths, leaving behind them a pair of small hands dotted brown with "tobacco juice," hands that trembled with the memory of the grasshopper's feet scratching skin. A benign creature, the grasshopper. Or so it seemed to me. As many grasshoppers as I'd seen in my short lifetime, still, I'd never witnessed an invasion. The last big hopper invasion had occurred in 1937, the year of my birth.

There is nothing benign about an incursion of grasshoppers, a phenomenon that occurs regularly on the Great Plains. Every seven years, say some hopper watchers, but others claim that the really big invasions come only every twenty years or so and coincide with cycles of drought, such as we experienced in the summer of 1988. When the hoppers come, they come en masse, flying so closely together that their combined bodies form a gray cloud that moves in from the horizon, accompanied by "a curious fluttering hum that seemed of the earth and the air, and a shimmering in the sun that came from millions of wings." Slowly the grasshoppers begin to drop down out of the sky until every small branch, every twig, every leaf trembles and bends beneath their weight, according to writer Mari Sandoz. Such huge swarms as these typically travel early in the day. Some clouds are so vast that they partially obscure the sun. At night, the swarms are sometimes attracted by the lights in house windows and streets. They come into town, as one swarm came into Alma, Nebraska, in 1935, and settle on street lights, on porches, in business houses, or any place where a light had been left burning. Businessmen were forced to close windows and doors—or else turn off their lights and retire for the night. Filling stations were particularly hard hit. Hoppers covered one filling station light pole so thickly the pole was nearly invisible under the swarm of moving bodies. The grasshoppers spread like blankets across well-lit intersections and driveways, and clung to the sides of buildings until daybreak when, once again, they moved on in search of food, fanning out over the residential sections of town and eventually retreating to the country-side.

The swarming masses of grasshoppers that invaded the Great Plains during the 1930s were certainly not the first of the hordes. Early travelers and explorers wrote of encountering swarms of hoppers so thick that they had to be beaten off of faces and arms, and early immigrants in the central plains area certainly had to cope with the critters. Between 1857 and 1875, grasshoppers invaded Nebraska eight times. The biggest raid was from July 20 to 22, 1874, when billions of hoppers covered the entire frontier of Nebraska, Kansas, the Dakotas, and Minnesota. So many insects invaded that the sun was darkened and the vibration of hopper wings made a roaring sound like the rushing of a storm. This roaring was followed by a deep hush as the hoppers dropped to the earth and began devouring the crops. Farmers who had risen to green fields at sunrise saw their crops reduced to stumps by night as hoppers struggled for the last bite. Insects stripped gardens. They gnawed holes through carpets and rugs that had been spread on fields to save the plants. They ate buds and bark off of fruit trees. They followed potatoes and onions right down into the earth, and ate wheat and oats in shock and wild grass in unplowed fields. The earth was covered with a gray mass of struggling, biting hoppers.

Settlers were helpless against this horde. Some of them ran out to flail at the hoppers with sacks or with hoes; some of them tried to eradicate the insects by using smudges and fire; and some, according to Sandoz, "lifted their faces into the dropping, crawling hail and cursed or prayed, according to their nature." Nothing did any good. Milk cows stampeded. Train wheels spun on the track from the grease of dead hoppers' bodies. Teams of horses bolted in the fields as swarms of hoppers flew into their faces with each step. Some women cried as they saw their flower gardens disappear, some screamed, and some sat in "brooding silence that was not to be broken for days, in one case almost a year."

During their stay, the grasshoppers "devoured everything

green and when this was gone, they forgot their color preference and ate almost anything regardless of color," reported the Orleans (Neb.) *Centennial*. Reports of the hoppers' ability to eat anything became greatly exaggerated. "Mike Manning said they ate the scranes off the windows," reported one journalist in 1874, while his 1936 counterpart spun the following tale: "A farmer near here had grasshoppers so thick that while making one round the other day they had ate up his pants clear to the knee, three of them had hold of the seat trying to pull them off, while one had the pliers out of the tool box doing his best to unfasten his belt. He said as fast as the bundles came from the binder a bunch of hoppers would grab it, carry it over in the shade, and eat to their heart's content.

"He couldn't even grease the machine for every time he opened up a bucket of axle grease they would rush him, grab the pail and smear it over themselves to prevent sunburn. He tried to solve the problem by importing a flock of turkeys, but that didn't prove out so well. They got so full of the insects they could do nothing but hop, which wasn't fast enough to prevent them from dying of sunstroke after the pesky things had pulled out all their feathers.

"He next tried cutting at night, thinking the hoppers couldn't see, but the crop destroyers hired a flock of lightning bugs and made a regular picnic of the occasion as they could work so much faster when it was cooler.

"The last we heard of him he was headed back north after a calf they had carried away while his back was turned. His wife had barricaded herself and children in the cellar and the hoppers are having a great time playing war, shooting darts at one another made from the shingles of the house."

It was common knowledge, though, that the hoppers would chew on the wooden handles of farm implements until the handles were rough. My father told of having, as a farm boy, laid down a hoe long enough to go into the house and eat his noonday meal only to find, on his return, the handle well chewed where his sweaty palms had touched it. His story is confirmed by Roy Glandt, who says of the hoppers of the 1930s, "There were millions of them. I remember when we stacked hay, we had to put the pitchforks under cover when we went to lunch. If you didn't, the grasshoppers would gnaw the handles to the point they'd be rough to grip by the time we got back. There was something about the salt from sweaty hands that seemed to attract them." Mrs. Grace Phipps, remembering the same time on a 160-acre farm near Plainview, Nebraska, said, "You'd hang clothes out and before they'd dry, the grasshoppers would eat them full of holes."

The invasions of the 1870s were so severe that many of the pioneers left the Great Plains. "Eaten out by grasshoppers. Going back east to live with wife's folks," read a sign painted on the canvas of one wagon. Those that stayed had to contend with another batch of hoppers the following year, for the female hoppers laid eggs in the soil. They would pierce the earth with holes and then fill the holes with eggs. Each female would lay about a hundred eggs and then die, so that the ground, covered with dead bodies, didn't signal rejoicing but only trouble ahead next year. When the little hoppers hatched, they hatched in the millions. They couldn't fly, but could only hop, so the settlers made ditches and drove the little creatures into them to die. Or they would lay rows of straw in a field and set the rows on fire after the hoppers had crawled in the straw to keep warm. Or they would drag shallow pans of kerosene across the fields for the nymphs to hop into. On the settlers' side was a cold, rainy spring that froze many of the little hoppers; the migrant birds, flying up from the south, stopped to feast on the insects as well. For the next two or three years, the plains were plagued with hoppers, and then they disappeared.

The grasshoppers that ate their way across the Great Plains in the 1870s were Rocky Mountain grasshoppers with slender bodies and light gray wings. They were at home on the high plains and in the Rocky Mountain foothills, but during the dry years when there was not enough food to sustain them in their natural habitat, they began to migrate to the east and the south in swarms. They would travel for hundreds of miles, sometimes flying all night before settling down in the late afternoon to rest and feed. When the hoppers finally lifted to fly on to their next spot, they left behind no leaf or gnawable branch, but only brush as bare as it is in the wintertime and rows of holes to show where carrots and turnips had been growing. Only their natural enemies — chickens, pheasants, and wild turkeys — benefited from their stay, gorging on the insects.

Calculating the extent of the damage done in those early years is difficult, but from 1936 to 1938 in Nebraska alone, farmers lost some $11 to $12 million annually from the hordes. Since a grasshopper consumes its own weight in food each day, according to the United States Department of Agriculture, eight or nine grasshoppers per square yard eat as much as a cow and a calf would eat in a summer. It was as though enormous herds were suddenly consuming the crops. More than eight grasshoppers per square yard is considered an infestation on range land, but when infestations get bad, grasshopper counts can run as high as thirty to eighty per square yard. In 1958, in Colorado, the state saw almost $60 million in crop losses from infestation. Hoppers "slit the leaves off and chew through the wheat stalks, just below the head, then the head drops," explains Ralph Hallock, a Sheridan Lake, Colorado, farmer. "They eat the ears off the barley so the barley won't pollinate, so no grain. They eat the silk off the corn, so no corn on the cob."

In the 1930s, the methods for dealing with the hoppers had gotten more sophisticated. Instead of dragging pans of kerosene across the fields, farmers bought poisoned bait at fifteen cents a sack and mixed it with a bran mixture that could be purchased from a county agent or made from scratch with chemicals from the drugstore. This would be spread over the fields. Some poultry and domestic animals were poisoned from the bran mixture, feeding on it in its unspread state or eating lumps or chunks of the stuff after it was spread. By 1958, chemical sprays had replaced the poisoned bran mixture as the preferred method of killing grasshoppers. Today, some of the most effective sprays, namely DDT and Dieldrin, have been outlawed, but spraying continues with costs shared between the farmer and the state or federal government.

"A grasshopper sitting on a sweet 'tater vine" makes for a jolly song. Two grasshoppers sitting on a sweet 'tater vine make for good fishing—the grasshopper makes an excellent bait for some fish. Six grasshoppers perched on a vine could be the beginnings of an appetizer for supper, according to Jerry Bell of the federal Animal Plant Health Inspection Service in Lincoln, Nebraska. "You can boil them in peanut oil and eat them," he says. "I'm told they're quite high in protein." But eight grasshoppers sitting on a sweet 'tater vine—"oh my, oh my"—signal the beginnings of a natural disaster, a plague of grasshoppers, an upsetting of the usual ecological balance, heralded by dry conditions that herald not only drought but grasshoppers on the move, eating their way across the breadbasket of America.

The Dust Storms

And the sun became black as sackcloth of hair.
— REVELATION 6:12

There's something medieval about the Great Plains. Partly it's the land, so flat and so immense, spread out like a wall-to-wall carpet from the Rockies to the Mississippi, from Canada to the Gulf of Mexico. Such a land can make one believe that the world itself is flat again, its four quarters perfectly balanced by the four cardinal directions, its one God safely ensconced in a zodiac heaven held up by the pitchforks of Justice, Prudence,

Huge black turbulent dust clouds overpower a small midwestern community, one of many. Courtesy Nebraska State Historical Society.

Temperance, and Fortitude. And partly it's the Gothic sky vaulting overhead, a sky even more expansive than the land. Thunder and lightning can play tag across this sky without crowding the sun; cumulus clouds can pile up like mountain ranges, yet fail to blot out its blue. Here the age-old litany of the wind, the "persistent, mournful crying wind of the plain," as Hamlin Garland put it, blows impartially on the just and the unjust. Here the single eye of the sun, blazing indifferently on good and evil, is rarely out of sight. Under such a sky, time itself seems eternal.

The immutability of the Great Plains, its vastness, the stark emptiness of so much undifferentiated space, is awesome, or would be if the Settler hadn't divvied up the land in such a simple, mathematical way: a plain geometry, as it were. Rectangular states right-angle one another, then break into checkerboards of counties, which separate into identical square-mile townships, which section into acres, which divide, ultimately, into cornfields — or occasionally multiply into a town that is halved by its Main Street and then subdivided into dozens of identical blocks, lots, and yards. Such simplicity, such thoroughness, seems in itself medieval.

Small wonder, then, that when the dust storms of the 1930s rolled over the plains, their turbulent black clouds pitching and heaving thundersqualls that showered dust instead of rain, some feared they were witnessing the apocalypse. The land, which had seemed so clearly defined, began to move: from field to field, from county to county, from state to state. The distinction between land and sky, once so clear, became blurred as earth rose up like an avenging angel of death to dance before the wind in a dozen different guises, as earth, on those rare windless days when nothing stirs, fell ominously from the sky, as thousands of tons of soil, once indisputably wed to the land, rose and invaded the stratosphere. Such a reversal of the physical world was shocking.

Few feared the end of the world more than a boy like Oscar Siefken, old enough to be working a team of horses in a field next to the cemetery when an early storm hit Nebraska in May, 1933, but still young enough to be uncertain of the future.

Clouds bearing dust—and static electricity—blackened the sky so rapidly that Oscar could barely see to unhitch the team. When he looked up from the harness, he blanched: blue balls of fire were spinning to the extremities of the cemetery's windmill wheel, exploding when lightning flashed, then reappearing as flames dancing like candles on the barbed-wire fence. Is it the dead rising? he wondered as he fled for home, leaving the horses behind him. Nothing else he knew explained it. A few miles away, Edna Robert hurried, along with most of her Champion, Nebraska, neighbors, into a potato cave to escape what looked like a thunderstorm. When the wind died down a few hours later, the townspeople emerged to find the sun glowing like a cannonball in a fiery red sky, a sky reddened from dirt falling through silent air. Edna was astounded. What could it portend? She put out her hands to receive the earth. It was coarse and rough—and filled with seeds.

But as each early storm passed, the sense of the apocalyptic died away with the wind. Dust storms, folks reminded themselves, are a normal part of life on the plains, where dry weather and high winds traditionally combine to shift soil, where the Settler complained in the 1800s about storms that left him sooty as a coal miner, where Indian villages were buried in dust as long ago as the fifteenth century, and where, eons earlier, the fertile loess itself had been blown in from the Rocky Mountains. In retrospect, it hardly seems remarkable that most people chose to dismiss the storms. There was something so arbitrary about them, so capricious. No two were quite alike. Some rolled in as magnificently as thunderheads; others shrieked in like relentless tidal waves. Some crept in like fog, clinging insidiously to the ground, then swelling until sky and land fused into a brownish pall. Others fell in a second, a pitch-black blanket unfurling, a thick whirling cloud of dust dark enough to turn day into midnight. Still, when the first of the great dust storms hit in November of 1933, even hardened newsmen were impressed. Originating in the Saskatchewan province of Canada and driven by gale-force winds, the storm swept through the Dakotas and Iowa, blackened faces of World's Fair visitors in Chicago and, the next day, turned New York skies yellow, its afternoon to dusk. "Much Awe Aroused by Phenomenon," headlined the *Journal* in Sioux City, Iowa, where the storm paled the eye of the bright afternoon sun until it shone as weird and blue as a foreign moon. The *Journal's* page-one story opened with a quote from Revelation. Anything less seemed inappropriate.

Indeed, anything short of Revelation would have been inappropriate, for the dust storms of the 1930s ended an era on the plains. They put an end to the world of the independent Farmer, a world based on a dream as reckless as the vision that drew miners, in 1849, across the prairie to the promised land beyond. The Farmer's dream, like the gold miners', was based on optimism and an indifference to the land. The dust storms that blew this world apart were themselves the result of a long process of disintegration, a process that began the moment the Settler sowed his first crop on the flat grasslands. But in 1933 the end was not yet visible — for dust storms, although more dramatic than drought when viewed as individual phenomena, actually extract their toll the same way: slowly, over the passage of time, like the embrace of a giant python whose coil tightens a bit more each week.

The dream that would tear the fertile land of the Great Plains into dust was an ancient dream, a dream of paradise that traces its lineage to the Garden of Eden, a dream that was already old when it drew Columbus to the new world. The Farmer inherited this dream as he inherited his land from immigrant ancestors who, when they crossed the Mississippi, found a flat empty space that encouraged their dream the way a desert evokes mirage. They were hardly alone. The first European to set foot on the plains was Coronado, following his vision of a kingdom of silver and gold. Wave after wave of Europeans followed. None was able to gaze upon the land and see it for what it was. Instead, like blind men, each discovered his own elephant.

Early explorers in 1820 were convinced that they saw a wasteland. So strong was their vision that the first maps marked the plains as the Great American Desert and, as late as 1859,

Horace Greeley wrote, "I judge that the desert is steadily enlarging its borders and at the same time intensifying its barrenness." He proclaimed this land unfit for human habitation. Those whose eyes were filled with dreams of fur or gold saw the plains, as many still do, as a vast thoroughfare linking east and west. They beat a pathway through prairie grass high enough to cover the backs of their horses; their tracks can still be seen, running parallel with Interstate 80. The Government, which fancied it could see the plains clearly from its vantage point in Washington, noted that the land looked a lot like Europe, laid out in modest European-sized farms of about 160 acres each. The Homestead Act, passed in 1862, made this vision official. Actually, the prairie was hardly comparable to any land in Europe; it was more like the great plains of China or Russia's vast steppes. But the Government's eyes were too full of the future to be able to see that.

Shrewdest dreamer of all was the Railroad, which saw nothing but coast-to-coast customers. It talked the Government into donating 400 feet of right-of-way plus ten (later twenty) sections of land for each mile of track. The Atchison, Topeka, and Santa Fe line alone received 3 million acres of public land this way. Then the Railroad, in true American style, set out to market its dream, launching such an effective advertising campaign that millions of farmers, looking for greener pastures, poured into the plains. They came from states east of the Mississippi River and they came from Europe, particularly from Ireland, Germany, and Scandinavia. Between 1870 and 1900, more acres were settled than had been during the country's entire previous history—some 430 million. The Railroad worked this miracle by financing newspapers which printed glowing stories about opportunities on the prairie, the newsprint transforming every little hamlet into a burgeoning metropolis. Railroad agents, well supplied with newspapers and with exhibition cars displaying plains produce, combed the East Coast and the cities of Europe. Europeans willing to migrate were given steamship tickets and a free hitch on the railroad halfway across the continent to the plains where, according to the agents, a husband waited for every woman, a thriving farm for every man. No wonder the Settler arrived with his eyes full of Eden.

Railroad, Government, and Settler all viewed the land, ultimately, the same way: as an object. Nature was undeniably "other." The land, per se, was foreign to them. It had no value except as inert matter upon which they could work their wills. Intrinsic meaning? The thought was absurd. They were men who believed that if a tree falls in the forest without a person to hear it, there would not only be no sound but no tree and no forest as well. This anthropocentric view of nature, this indifference to the land itself, was central to the dream that the Farmer inherited.

When the Settler arrived in his well-advertised Eden, he was greeted by an old-timer who looked at his ax and scoffed, "A grass sickle will chop down all the trees where you're going." It was virtually true. The promised land was a shadeless plain, with not enough trees to build a fire let alone a house, and with water more scarce than shade. The Settler burned buffalo chips, built his house of sod, and nearly broke his back trying to till the promised land. True, he didn't have to fell a tree or move a boulder to clear his field, but the very soil itself resisted the plow. Indeed, it broke the fragile European blade the Settler had brought with him; he had to resort to the John Deere plow in order to break sod and, even then, it took five oxen to pull the steel blade through the ground and transform the flat land of paradise into farmland. The virgin prairie grass had root systems extending deep into the ground, searching the subsoil for moisture. The root network for each clump of grass totalled a mile or more. It wove, beneath the surface of the land, a web as thick and brown as a thrush's nest, a web that knitted land and plant and had for centuries. The Settler, in plowing, didn't simply break sod; he broke root — and in breaking root, he began to break the land's defense system against the prairie wind.

The land, in turn, nearly broke the Settler's dream. It didn't yield the way moist European soil had. Even 160 acres of choice land (and homesteading land was rarely choice) was not enough to support a man. The Settler had to purchase decent land from the Railroad or from real-estate promoters who bought land in large blocks, then resold it by the acre. As if that weren't tribulation enough, there was always the weather, hardly paradisical. If hot sun and high wind didn't drive folks mad in summer, then winter blizzards would. Or hail. Or grasshopper plagues. Or prairie fires. No wonder settlers left the plains in droves, as many as ninety percent abandoning some areas. Signs on returning prairie schooners cryptically summed it up: "In God we trusted; in Kansas we busted." But despite afflictions, settlement crept steadily westward, following diminishing rainfall—about thirty-two inches annually at Dubuque, Iowa, thirty-one at Des Moines, twenty-six at Omaha. By the turn of the century, most land was occupied. East of the 98th meridian, which nearly splits the plains in half, farmers tilled the land, harvesting cash crops of wheat and corn, gardening, raising chickens and hogs, and grazing cattle, for American farming was still diversified in the European fashion—a realization of the Government's dream. To the west of the 98th meridian where annual precipitation of about twenty inches makes farming unprofitable, ranchers grazed cattle and cursed the Farmer who, they maintained, was the ruin of the country, having "everlastingly, eternally, now and forever, destroyed the best grazing land in the world."

Meanwhile the Settler's dream, weakened but not abandoned, was unexpectedly shored up for the Farmer by a new dream forming in the east, a sophisticated belief in progress that would replace America's naive trust in providence. Progress, after all, rested not on myth but on an inviolable law of nature. It was scientific. Darwin's *On the Origin of Species* began to assume an authority once claimed only by the Bible, and lo, the ancient dream of Eden began to transform itself into an optimistic vision of a utopian future based on science and technology, a new civilization whose unfolding was as inevitable as man's evolution from the apes.

World War I rapidly advanced this dream. "Wheat will win the War," the Government proclaimed when the beastly Hun blockaded the Dardanelles, cutting Europe off from her Russian wheat basket. "Plant wheat." The market place echoed the cry: wheat prices jumped from a prewar level of $0.60 to $0.80 a bushel, jumped to $1.00, then to $1.40, and kept rising. By 1917, when the United States entered the war, wheat had broken $2.00, the highest price the Farmer had ever received. It went up to $2.10 and held. As the market boomed, the industrialist — smelling profit — took time off from developing tanks to do for the tractor what Henry Ford had done for the automobile: turn it from a novelty to a necessity. When salesmen showed the Farmer how, if he replaced his team of horses with a fuel-powered tractor, he could plant as much as he could reap, the Farmer didn't need much convincing. The number of cultivated acres doubled during the war as tractors rolled onto the plains by the thousands. More than 11,000,000 acres — or twice the land area of Massachusetts — was land that had been plowed for the first time. In Kansas alone, wheat acreage increased from 4,870,000 acres in 1910 to nearly 12,000,000 in 1919. Even the weather cooperated. The sky sent down a plentiful rainfall, which combined with patriotism, profits, and technology to create an era of prosperity such as the Farmer had never known. The settler's old dream of a land of plenty seemed to be coming true. Of course the Farmer, his head full of progress, credited technology: it was magic; it had turned the Farmer into an alchemist who could transform the base substance of the earth into tiny seeds of pure gold.

The end of the war should have collapsed the market and the dream of progress, but it did not. Instead, the Government guaranteed wheat prices as part of its relief to Europe. And, by the time Europe had recovered, the industrialist had come up with a new technological miracle: the combine. This marvelous new machine which cut, threshed and cleaned the grain, released the Farmer from his dependence on the hired hand in exactly the same way that the tractor had released him from his dependence on the horse. The ceiling went off wheat production; the age of wheat kings began. Between 1925 and 1930, the amount of cultivated land jumped by thirty-four percent. With the combine, the Farmer could reap as much as he could plant. With the tractor, he could plant as much as he could plow. With both, a bushel of wheat took only three minutes of human labor to produce. There was one drawback: it took a lot of land to make a combine pay. But the Industrialist offered easy terms, and the Banker volunteered to mortgage farmland. No slacker, the Farmer borrowed, bought land, and began to plow up everything he could. First he plowed farm land, then he plowed pasture. Everywhere he planted wheat, which left fields bare from the sowing to the sprouting of the seed. Winter wheat was the worst: sown in the fall, it left fields bare to the wind all winter long. When the Farmer ran out of land on the rainy eastern half of the 98th meridian, he crossed right over into semiarid ranchland and plowed that, too, gambling on rain as he replaced long-rooted prairie grass with short-rooted wheat. He staked his dream against the soil for, by the time he finished sowing, the only thing that remained to bind dirt to land was moisture. So blinded was he by his dream that he even tilled land whose topsoil was so thin that the plains clay, caliche, lay just below the bite of the plow. The sky was the limit, as far as the Farmer was concerned. It never occurred to him that the land might have a limit, too.

Had the Farmer had a better sense of history, he might have recalled that a similar combination of factors—profit motive, modern technology, and indifference to nature—had combined in the late 1800s to exterminate roughly 40 million buffalo in two years' time, rendering them all but extinct. The price for buffalo hides in 1871 and 1872, when this happened, was excellent, particularly considering that hunters didn't have to buy or raise the beasts. Railroad provided the transportation; the Sharps rifle with its telescopic sight provided the means. The hunter killed the way the Farmer plowed—indiscriminately. A good sharpshooter with a little luck could drop a hundred animals before the herd would stampede. The hunter was limited only by his skinner, who often worked from dawn to dusk struggling to keep pace with the gun, and who often left carcasses behind to rot under the hot prairie sun, creating such a stench that travelers couldn't help but notice it. That the fertile topsoil of the plains is not, today, entirely extinct is due to the difference between the nature of the buffalo and the nature of the land, not to any essential difference in man's relationship to them.

But the Farmer, busy sowing wheat and reaping gold, could foresee no end to this land of milk and honey. Never, in fact, had his dream seemed more real. Progress was visible everywhere: in radio waves which brought New York to his living room; in the automatic planters which seeded his crops; in the towering silos made of gleaming concrete; in the dozens of cars and trucks zipping up and down the roadways; in the streamlined trains tearing across the continent; in the planes overhead, bucking air currents on a new frontier.

Then, in 1930, drought hit. Precipitation east of the Rockies that summer was 500 billion tons short of normal — the worst drought on record, the weather bureau said. It lifted in 1931, dropped again in 1932, and by 1934 looked likely to run forever. The hot eye of the sun, beating endlessly down, began to evaporate the land's final protection against the wind — moisture. Lakes dried to puddles, and the water table under the plains, which feeds the area's wells, lowered perceptibly. In Nebraska, where I was born, the Platte River was nothing but one long sandbar cutting across the state. That was hardly unusual (hadn't Artemus Ward called the Platte "a good river if you set it on edge"?) but sandbars in the Mississippi River were disconcerting. The Mississippi dropped to an all-time low, 2.5 feet below its previous low-water mark of 1864, so shallow in spots that swimmers could walk across the channel. "So durn dry the carp'll have to grow wings to survive," the Farmer joked, but it wasn't funny when fish, trapped in sloughs, began to die. Nor did Grace Phipps laugh when drought split open cracks in the baked earth so wide that her cow, stepping in one, broke its leg.

Still, the Farmer was hardly alone in his lack of foresight. When a 1933 thunderhead dropped red dirt mixed with rain, an imaginative Nebraska newsman wrote: "Omaha was blanketed with thick, red volcanic dust early this morning. It is believed to have been carried from volcanic eruptions in the Aleutian Islands several weeks ago." A University of Nebraska geology professor, E. E. Schramm, was more realistic. When he analyzed the dust (gypsum, volcanic ash, silt particles), he concluded that it originated in the red Permian beds of Kansas, Oklahoma, or Texas, beds formed late in the Paleozoic Era (before the rise of the dinosaur) and now, some 250 million years later, transported by wind to Nebraska. Yet even Professor Schramm was unwilling to see what this might mean. Instead, he considered the dust storm a windfall: hadn't Nebraska farmers just received $25 million worth of free fertilizer?

Optimism was endemic. Journalists, railroad officials, and chamber of commerce secretaries joined the professor in being jolly in the face of the storms. When dust blew thick enough to blur the outline of a person sitting across the room, they joked about the ingenious chap who, loath to clean house, decided to plant his garden indoors. Or about the clever bachelor who harnessed wind-driven dust ripping through his keyhole by holding pots and pans in front of it, blasting them spic and span. When an occasional rain splattered against the dry earth, they would enthusiastically herald the return of prosperity. When prosperity failed to return, they occupied themselves by identifying sources of dust—a regional sport. Yellow dust could be traced to the grazing lands of Texas and New Mexico, brown dust was fertile dirt from western Kansas, while black dust (actually clay particles) came from South Dakota or Canada. "Welp," they joked during storms, "your uncle should be along any minute now. There goes his farm."

This blind optimism was not confined to the Plains. When the first great dust storm reached the East Coast in November, 1933, the *New York Times* was quick to assure readers there was no need to worry. Such storms, wrote its science writer Waldemar Kaempffert, are similar to the red sirocco storms of Europe, which blow across the Mediterranean from the Sahara Desert, storms that sometimes combine with rain to form "showers of blood" which occasionally strike terror in the hearts of superstitious peasants. These displays are nothing compared with the record dustfall of March, 1901, a series of cyclones that dropped some 550 million tons of dust over much of North

Africa, the Mediterranean, and western Europe, transporting dirt some 2,500 miles. Which, in turn, was peanuts beside the volcanic eruption of Krakatoa, which shot dust 50 miles into the air, turned skies red for three days over much of the world's surface, and rained dust around the globe for years. Now that was a dustfall.

As time passed and the storms loomed larger, as they increased in frequency and intensity, repeatedly darkening not only the plains but the East Coast, depositing precious "fertilizer" not only on prairie farmland but on New York City sidewalks, they became harder and harder to dismiss. Still, nearly everyone managed to: optimism formed a cataract on the national eye. Scientists dismissed the storms by transforming them into statistics: 308,950 dust particles per cubic foot (eighty percent of them loam) were counted in Chicago's loop during a storm (and compared with a normal Chicago count of 120,000). Geologists reduced the storms by telling how the vast plains of China were formed from wind-blown dust or by quoting a saying (which, of course, couldn't be proven) that every square mile of the earth's surface contains at least one speck of dust from every other. Newsmen, concerned about the bad press that dust was getting, turned eloquent: dust makes the rain fall, it makes the sky blue, it steeps the heavens in purple and red at eventide, it shields us from the fierce effulgence of the sun. Pilots, bucking the storm clouds on behalf of the scientists, bacterial plates strapped to the sides of their speeding cabin planes, vacuum tubes and suction devices dangling from their windows, transformed the storms into adventures that were reduced, by wags, to the story about a pilot who, forced to bale out of his plane during a dust storm, spent six hours shoveling his way to earth.

The storms were regarded as "freaks of nature," weird combinations of circumstances that couldn't possible be repeated in a hundred years. "Blood rains" were considered oddities that could only be relegated — along with showers of frogs and periwinkles — to the columns of Ripley's "Believe It or Not." And, in truth, there was something fantastic about a dust cloud that covered 1,350,000 square miles and stood three miles high, that stretched from Canada to Texas, from Montana to Ohio, a cloud so colossal it obliterated the sky. Just as there was something preternatural about a dust cloud dense enough to eclipse the sun simultaneously in six states. Or about New Mexico's soil turning New England snow yellow. Or about a four-day storm, this one in May, 1934, that transported some 300 million tons of dirt 1,500 miles, from the Rocky Mountains to the Eastern seaboard, that darkened New York, Baltimore, and Washington for five hours, and that dropped dust not only on the President's desk in the White House but also on the decks of ships some 300 miles out in the Atlantic. Who could believe such things?

Certainly not the Farmer. After each storm, he paused to curse his bad luck, then revved up his tractor, drove to his windblown fields, and replanted his crop. A man of dreams, the Farmer was, and a man of fierce determination. Doggedly he plowed the dry earth, keeping one eye on the profit he was bound to reap when it rained and the other on the plume of dust that rose behind his tractor. He had to replant. He owed the Banker so much it was reap wheat or lose his farm, so he ignored the county agent's warnings against "reckless sodbusting" as they'd been ignored since the late 1800s. And he paid no attention to the Government that begged him to stop plowing, that had beseeched him, since 1929, to reduce his wheat acreage. Why should he listen? Government subsidy, even under the Hoover administration, kept the wheat market from foundering. Instead, the Farmer plowed like a man determined to make a silk purse out of a sow's ear, no matter what the price. So strong was his dream and so keen his optimism he refused to believe that he was laboring only for the wind. But he was. Each turning of the earth only pulverized the soil further, leaving it more prone to blow. Topsoil, cream of the earth, went first. When the wind came in, hugging the ground, dry dust rose like a mist, whipped into a froth as fine as soap suds, skimmed over the land, cutting from one field to another until both surfaces were moving. Not just earth went. So did humus, separated from the soil by the wind; so did seed, blown out of the furrows, and small plants, lifted bodily into the air. Little remained grounded, finally, but barren soil—and the roots of growing grain which, exposed to the hot eye of the sun, would soon wither and die. The more conscientious the Farmer had been, the more he pulverized the soil in plowing, the greater his loss.

The more the dust blew, the finer it became, grinding itself into smaller and smaller particles until it hung in the air like motes in a sunbeam. It blew everywhere, penetrating even closed houses, rippling on window sills, obscuring upholstery patterns, clinging to walls and curtains. Nothing could shut it out. The housewife tried, of course. She stuffed oiled rags around windows and doors; when that didn't work, she sealed cracks with packing tape; when that didn't work, she hung bedsheets and sprayed them with water or kerosene. But nothing worked. Food laid out for supper would be ruined, the milk turned black in the glass. Everything—beds, clothes in the closet, food in the refrigerator—was covered with a fine film. Dust seasoned every edible thing, except maybe soft-boiled eggs or food from a can. Even pillows smelled acrid, an odor that would linger for days. Faced with layers of dust on carpet and floor, inches of dust piled in bathtub and sink, the housewife cleaned with shovel and bucket, not broom, only to repeat the process each time the wind rose. More and more dust blew, dense mists rising like the spray of ocean breakers and hanging so thickly over the road that headlights couldn't penetrate the powder-fine haze, and the motorist couldn't see the radiator cap on his own automobile. "It takes grit to live in this country," joked the Farmer, but few laughed as masses of dust began to billow into huge tumbling clouds, as black as ebony at the base and muddy tan at the top, some so saturated with fine dust particles that ducks and geese, caught in flight, suffocated; some swelling and spreading until the sun struggled at midday, to penetrate the dust-laden cloud, until the sun paled, turned into a metallic orb, and disappeared; some turning the sky so black that chickens, thinking it night, would roost.

The storms were not perpetual, but they began to seem that way. "There is rarely a day when at some time dust clouds do not roll over," wrote Caroline Henderson, an Oklahoma farm woman, for the *Atlantic Monthly*. Oklahoma counted 102 storms in the span of one year; North Dakota reported 300 in eight months' time. Most arrived early in the day and lasted until nightfall, but some raged through the night, and a few blew for days. The devastation wreaked by these "black blizzards" was astounding. Some 300,000 square miles — or four times the land area of Nebraska — were damaged by dust or erosion. The Government estimated that 850 million tons of soil were being swept off the plains each year, leaving some 150,000 square miles of land devoid of topsoil, bleak stretches of ground that lay totally barren beneath the wind. After the blizzards, people crept from houses or storm cellars to view a world increasingly transformed. Dead rabbits and birds littered the fields; once-green gardens and pastures lay beneath carpets of dust so fine that shoes left tracks as though in snow. Landmarks disappeared: plum thickets died out, even groves of locust trees vanished. Anything that slowed the wind — a tractor, a tumbleweed caught in barbed wire — would have a drift behind it. Dirt covered fence lines until only scattered post tops remained visible; it drifted as high as eaves of houses; it blocked roads and railroad tracks so badly that snow plows had to clear them.

A kind of terror grew in people. Fear of dust pneumonia increased as deaths from respiratory diseases mounted. In March, 1935, Dr. R. F. Patterson figured that perhaps a hundred people in Baca County, Colorado, were walking around with dust pneumonia — or "brown lung," as it was called. Four had died of it. People tied layers of wet cheesecloth across their faces, put vaseline in their nostrils, tucked children in bed with wet towels draped across their heads, but there was no way not to inhale dust, not to taste it, not to grind its grit in your teeth. Red Cross masks caught some, nostril hairs and bronchial mucus stopped more, but in the end the fine dust drifted past everything. Being in a storm was something like working at the tailend of a strawstacker in a loft — it cut off breathing. People feared being caught outdoors where they were no better off than the beasts of the field who, blinded by dust, would run in circles until they dropped from exhaustion and died of asphyxiation.

A man and two boys flee a billowing Oklahoma storm that is showering dust. Photograph by Arthur Rothstein, April 1936. Courtesy Library of Congress.

One farmer, caught in his own ten-acre garden, wandered blindly for eight hours before he stumbled against the side of his house. Others followed fence rows home or crawled along town pavements on hands and knees, wearing clean through the capped toes of their Florsheim oxfords. A Kansas boy lost in a storm on his way home from school was found the next day buried in dirt. Other, more nameless terrors rose in the still of night, accompanied by the sound of dry fields cracking. "My husband and I would wake in a panic," remembers Ruby Boyer of Nebraska. "We used to walk the floors." Living things were no longer themselves. Desperate farmers bought water in town, hauled it home by the barrel, and hand-carried it to field and garden in bucket and cup—an exercise in futility, perhaps in madness. Lackluster cattle, which had fed on weeds, then on thistles, finally on nothing, stood gaunt and listless, their hides rough; ugly growths festered around their mouths. Some farmers offered livestock, free, to anyone who could feed them. One man, in Minnesota, shot twenty-two head of cattle, and then himself. Outside her Oklahoma home, Caroline Henderson found a starved and trembling jackrabbit, one eye battered out by dirt. He made no attempt to escape, so she bathed his eye and gave him shelter, asking herself what it means when wild creatures, normally so able to care for themselves, seek protection. Outlined against the sky, summer trees stood naked as skeletons, while farm houses seemed like strange summer cottages dotted along wind-rippled dunes of dust on a vacated beach. Except for the savage grandeur of the wind, the world was silent and desolate: most of the wildlife that hadn't been killed had already migrated.

Men followed suit. By 1935, thousands of dry-land farmers were streaming out of the plains in a great exodus to California that would be memorialized later by John Steinbeck. During the decade of the thirties, every state in the Union gained in population except five: the Dakotas, Nebraska, Kansas, and Oklahoma. Those states lost more than 300,000 people; most of them left in 1935 and 1936. Some folks — desperate, stubborn, or held tenaciously to the land by hope — stayed. "This ain't nothing new for most of us," the Farmer, dogged to the end, bragged. "I been busted six times before and I'm that way now." He paused, considered, and finally tempered his optimism: "Only you can't come back so easy any more." It was the truth. But when the Farmer had to buy food in town for the first time in his life — canned goods to see him through the winter instead of vegetables laid down in the cellar — he stopped boasting. Crop failure followed crop failure until life seemed as biblical as Revelation: "One woe is past; and behold, there come two woes more hereafter." Fields were badly eroded; some had lost topsoil as deep as the land had been plowed. The remaining subsoil — or clay, in some cases — was not porous enough to retain moisture or rich enough to support plants. Many, including the Government, feared that the Great Plains had become the Great American Desert that early explorers thought it was. Pasture after pasture was destitute of grass; corn field after corn field yielded nothing but dead stalks. "I don't think I picked ten bushels of corn from 320 acres," said Roy Glandt of a Nebraska crop. The land itself had lost its capacity to sustain life. The ocean of prairie grass that had been tamed into amber waves of grain became, in a few years, a wasteland. Even the hardy yucca plant, survivor of the desert's extremes, knuckled under, Caroline Henderson noted, its entire root system exposed by the wind, "thick woody roots writhing on the surface and the finger rootlets extending like guy wires for perhaps twenty feet in different directions." The plains had become a land where light is as darkness. Finally, even the Farmer's optimism crumbled into despair. "We drive as if going to a funeral," wrote Meridel Le Sueur of this period. "The corpse is the very earth."

And so it was. The dream of progress had proved to be not an alchemy but a black magic that had all but exterminated the land. Progress, with its technology, its profit motive, and its indifference to nature, had reduced paradise to a darkling plain. No longer could anyone believe that the earth would, necessarily, abide forever. That the land would, unconditionally, remain part of the land. No longer could man believe in his dominion. The shock was understandably extreme: it was the shock of the infant discovering the breast is not his. The lesson was a bitter one. The Farmer cursed his dream.

The long task of reclaiming the land began; the Government took most of the initiative. "Plant trees," said the Government, and thousands of trees were planted as windbreakers. "Dig ponds," said the Government, and ponds were dug. Snow fences were put up to slow wind erosion, dirt-filled burlap bags were piled on top of dunes, and emergency cover crops were sown. The Government purchased some 2 million acres (including 220,000 abandoned farms) and planted them with native grasses, retiring much of the land permanently from agricultural use. The reclamation process took four years, even with the help of rain. But eventually the plains healed, and crops grew again—not that the land would ever be the same. Topsoil, once blown away, can never be returned; virgin prairie, once plowed, can never be reclaimed. But gardens sprouted, lilacs and roses bloomed, and wildlife returned.

The dust storms had not been apocalyptic in a physical sense, but in another sense they were. We who were born, as I was, at the end of the thirties, were born into a new era. The Farmer was gone. He had been replaced by the Agronomist, a scientist of soil management who was concerned with regulating, not conquering, nature, who worked closely with the engineer to conserve the precious resources of the plains. The Agronomist, of course, believed in the survival of the fittest, but he was not as cocky as the Farmer had been, not as certain that man was destined to win that particular fray. In this new world, man and nature hung in a delicate balance. Accordingly, in the classrooms of the forties, I was taught (alongside the farm boys) the lessons of the thirties: how to reduce wind erosion by strip farming and by crop rotation, how to plow at right angles to the prevailing winds, how to conserve moisture by stubble mulching and by keeping a cover crop on dry land. We were taught a new respect for the ancient arts of terracing and contour farming; we were taught a new respect for the land. "He who is prudent in his use of the land," we were told, "will suffer only heavy losses during the cycles of drought, but he who is improvident will suffer disaster." Clearly the sins of our fathers were not meant to be repeated.

Outside the classroom, I watched these lessons being driven home as a huge dam was built on the Republican River that cuts across Nebraska south of the Platte, a dam designed to retain the water that flows across the plains from the Rocky Mountains, water that could irrigate the crops during the inevitable seasons of drought. It was part of a vast system of dams being carved into the plains. The age of reckless and fickle optimism was clearly over. The world that had begun the moment that the Settler and his piano-playing wife had arrived on the plains with his plow and his wagonload of dreams was gone. The dust storms had blown it away as surely as they had dispersed the topsoil, as surely as the wind had toppled the hardy independence of the Farmer and eroded his dream. Not even the energy of World War II could quite bring it back. It was history, buried with the buffalo. The sky, the enormous Gothic sky, still arched endlessly overhead, and underfoot the land stretched out, or so it seemed, from sea to sea. But that, we knew, was an illusion. The sky might be limitless, but the earth was not.

PART II

Air

Hail

"Gol durn it to hail," Grandpa Benjamin Franklin Coffey said. His words would be prophetic, but he had no way of knowing that. Instead, he looked ruefully down at his hand. That Boy Scout hatchet sure was as sharp as a whetstone could grind it; he hadn't even felt the blade go in! The ax had severed the web of his hand, between his index finger and his thumb. He picked his hand up. It was hurting now. He raised his arm in the air and started fumbling for his handkerchief to stop the bleeding; the cut was bleeding pretty free and his whole wrist was throbbing. June, his oldest boy, came up and understood instantly what had happened. "Here, Dad, use mine." He handed Ben his ban-

A combination of fact and fiction.

*Gol durn it to hail! Hail could wipe a year's crop out in a matter of minutes —
and did, in this corn field in 1896. Courtesy Nebraska State Historical Society.*

danna and went, without another word, to the team. He drove Ben home.

Clara gave a shriek when she saw her husband holding up what looked, for an instant, like a bloody stump. Then she calmed herself and began to analyze the situation so she could do what she had to do. Well, Ben's hand looked bad, but not as bad as June had looked the day he came running in from the neighbor's barn, his mouth a mass of blood. The day he had knocked his four front teeth out. Permanent teeth, not baby teeth. The durn fool. He and his brothers and the neighbor boys had been playing in the barn. There must of been a dozen of them, her six and the neighbor's six; they had made a ride out of hay slings. One boy would take a sling and pull it clear to one end of the barn and climb on; then another boy would climb up on a platform at the other end, grab the rope attached to the sling, and jump down. Those slings would come a-flying across the barn and June, he had to make a good thing better; he figured he would pull the rope, he was so much bigger and heavier than the other kids, being the oldest. He figured if he pulled the rope, that sling would come across in a real hurry. He was right about that, but he forgot to figure that he was taller, too. That sling caught him right in the mouth as it came across, the same day that one of the neighbor boys cut his hand so bad on the fence.

Clara helped Ben wash his hand and together they looked at it. She put some alum water on it, and Ben didn't even groan although she could see the alum water hurt by the way his breath had tightened and by the stiff way he held his chest. Alum helped congeal the blood; they both knew it was good. Then Clara went to her sewing box and selected her best thread — silk. The stitching took no time at all. Afterwards, Ben told her how it had happened, how he'd been splitting elm logs. She knew how hard elm logs were to split, didn't she? He had driven steel wedges in, but the wood had just splintered away. The steel wedges weren't wide enough, so he had been whittling out a wedge of wood, whacking first one side and then the other with that little hatchet when it happened, when he made a slip.

Like everyone else, Ben and Clara went to church on Sundays. A man could wear his coveralls to the country church, that is, if they were patched and washed brand-spanking-new clean. Speaking of clean overalls, Ben nearly snorted, reminded him of his brother George when George was still a kid. He'd been told to wash and clean up and put on a different pair of overalls so he'd look decent when he went to the neighbor's place on an errand. The overalls he was wearing had a hole in the seat. Well, George had thought that changing clothes was considerable trouble. He reasoned the matter out: he'd walk into the neighbor's house and then back out so no one would notice the place where the patch should be. His plan worked fine: he made it inside the door all right and had transacted his business and was backing out when he miscalculated. He missed the door by a few inches and sat down in a slop pail that was sitting there. Ben nearly snorted again. He wished that he could have seen George retreating, hole and slop and boy! He remembered the sheepish way George had come home and washed up without saying nothing. Ben swallowed, to keep from laughing out loud in church, and looked down at his own overalls, so clean, and something made him remember the picture he and his seven brothers had posed for so long ago, them duded up real fancy, wearing dark suits and ties and high white collars that framed their thick necks. He and Jack and Jim and Charley were all sitting on the front row. Every one of them had a mustache, and them three had watches; he remembered because they all sat with their jackets open so the boys' watch chains would show against their vests, and Ben's jacket open too, but no watch chain to show for it, not until his father, James, had died and left him his. That suit he had on was the last suit he'd owned; he never thought the day would come to this: he'd been unable to go to his son, June's, wedding because he didn't own a decent suit to wear. Now he thought being rich was not having to wear a pair of overalls with a patch in the back! Maybe he was thinking about the photograph because he and his boys had had their pictures taken when the boys were still young: quite a contrast, all of them with their dirty faces and tousled hair and shabby overalls, just as if they didn't own anything better, and Clara always had one dress she kept a little better than the others by not wearing it so regularly. It was cotton, but the color was fresh.

After church, a man by the name of Johnson cornered Ben and wanted to know what had happened to his hand, that it was all wrapped up, and Johnson wouldn't shut up until he had the whole story out of Ben, and when he did, he began laughing and razzing Ben to death. "We better send you back to the Boy Scouts, let them teach you how to use a hatchet," he crowed, and commenced to laugh again. Wouldn't you know it, the next week this man Johnson came to church with his hand wrapped up, and be durned if he hadn't cut his thumb plumb off. He was out cutting up wood — splitting wood, actually; he already had it cut up in short lengths. He put one piece on top of the other and then put his thumb on top, and durned if he didn't come right down and cut the end of his thumb off! "Johnson," Ben said, right in the middle of the church yard, "you durn old fool, you were going to send me back to the Boy Scouts, were you? Now I ask you, where in the hell are we going to send you?" And Ben threw back his head and laughed even though he could feel Clara's eyes tugging at his shirt sleeve. He knew what she'd say: "Watch your mouth, you ain't in the barnyard, Ben." She'd whisper it under her breath, talking to him in familiar language, the kind they spoke when they were alone although Clara could speak real good English. Damn right she could! Her father'd been a judge over to McCook and never mind that she'd been raised in a sod house, her mother taught her how to speak well, like a girl should. But she didn't put on airs with him.

Ben was a jovial man, but one thing certain, he was against the vote for women.

"What do you want the vote for?" he asked Clara. "You'll just go down and vote like I do. All it means is more votes for them to count."

Clara, who hardly weighed a hundred pounds soaking wet, heard him out, then asked, "How can you be so sure?"

Ben's brow wrinkled. "Of what?"

"That I'd vote like you do." Clara, née Smith, was the daughter of a politician herself. Her father, Isaac Matts Smith, had been an avid William Jennings Bryan man, and Clara took her politics seriously. She considered her vote beyond sale to anyone, even to her husband, although she would never dream of telling him that. Still, for an instant, she saw a flicker of doubt flash across his face. Then he grabbed her, in a bear hug: "I know you," he said. "I know you couldn't go up there and vote against me."

It was that ability to evoke a glimmer of uncertainty that marked a Coffey, that made Clara Grandma Coffey, not Grandma Smith. You never knew for sure if she were joking or for real. Ben was the same way. Sometimes the only way to find out was to test him out, but that could be dangerous. Clara remembered when their boys, "Pat" and Vic, were playing in the house. They were supposed to be doing dishes. Instead, they were arguing and fighting. Clara had told them a half a dozen times to cut it out and get to doing the dishes. Ben sat there and listened to it until he'd had enough, then he said, "All right. I believe you heard what your mother said. Let's get with it." Vic straightened up to go to work, but Pat wanted to make sure Ben meant what he said. So Pat said, "Well, scolding don't hurt, licking don't last long, and you don't dare to kill me." About that time Ben was on his feet and Pat was out the door, but Ben caught him before he made it to the road. Clara thought Ben did dare to kill Pat that night, but another night he might of been content to feint a cuff at the boy's ears. There was no way of telling.

Ben, like all the Coffeys, admired a good bluffer, someone who could take it as well as dish it out. That's why he loved his sister Nell; she could take a joke. His boys loved her, too. The last time Aunt Nell had stayed with them, the boys had given her quite a ride. Ben had this big old bulldog that the boys had broke to drive a little two-wheeled cart. He was strong enough to pull a person, and the boys would hook Old Towser up to that cart, and away they'd go. Well, as soon as Aunt Nell seen it, she wanted to ride in that cart with Towser pulling, but Towser was one of those dogs that likes to go into the horse tank after stuff and fish it out. You'd throw a brick or something into the horse tank, and he'd go in and feel around with his feet until he found the brick, and then down he'd go and fetch it out with his mouth. The boys set Aunt Nell up clear way out to the road, and when she and Old Towser were all set, why one of the boys ran for the horse tank with a brick in his hand and hollered, "Here, Towser." Well, that dog would rather jump in the horse tank than eat, so about that time, he just brought Aunt Nell to the horse tank a flying. Aunt Nell thought he'd stop, but the boy threw the brick right into the tank. Aunt Nell didn't go into the tank—she just rolled out there in the yard—but Towser and the cart went in.

Very rarely had Ben seen his sister's bluff called, but one time when she'd stayed over, he had. The issue was castor oil. That was Aunt Nell's cure-all. It didn't make any difference what in the world was the matter with you, castor oil would cure it. Well, when she'd stayed over that time, she'd gotten sick, she got really sick, and there were six boys in the household, each of whom had had to swallow that awful pale viscid medicine when he'd been in bed, and they insisted that it would cure her. "Oh, no, don't give me castor oil," she said. "I'll get up, I'll mop the floors, I'll do anything, just don't give me that castor oil." She meant it! She wouldn't touch the stuff.

Ben was a real jovial good-natured man until he got teed off. He didn't get teed off often, but when he did, look out! The last time was in town, in Stamford, Nebraska, where Ben always went to transact his business. This one guy in town kind of got under Ben's hide anyway. Ben was big. He stood six foot one in his stocking feet, and he weighed well over two hundred pounds, closer to three if the truth be known, and this guy, always, every time he saw Ben he'd walk up and punch him in the belly. Well, a fellow can take only so much of that and, even if you like a guy, it'll get old after awhile. And Ben didn't much like him, remember. Ben took it a long time, but he decided that he'd had enough. Boy, did he stop that in a hurry. He was a wild cat when he was teed off.

Horses diving into water tanks, men wrassling bears — such were the marvels of turn-of-the-century county fairs. This one at Alma, Nebraska, 1906.

Once he even wrassled a bear and won. My dad was just a little boy then, and he saw it all. The occasion, he told me, was a traveling carnival of the sort that went from town to town in those days with a fairly large-sized brown bear on a chain. The carnival managers would put up a price for the man who could wrassle the bear to the ground. So Grandpa Ben spit on his hands, once, for luck, and wiped them on the seat of his pin-striped overalls, and took his turn.

Ben was no fool. He let all the town's hot young bloods go first. He watched how the bear fought, and then he ambled on over to where the young bucks stood, and he listened to their descriptions of their fights: "And then, just when I thought I'd got him, there came that left paw of his out of nowhere."

The trick, Ben decided, was to grab the bear before the bear could grab him; the difficulty would be to ignore the crowd which would urge him to move before he was ready. Win or lose, at least he would know what it felt like to wrassle with one of the damn things, and he could count on the carnival managers to pull the beast off of him before it pawed him to death; the managers wouldn't want to be sued for manslaughter. So it wasn't as though he were risking his life. He made sure that June and Ray were there to see him, and his boys talk about the fight to this day, how he moved in so slowly that the crowd jeered him, how he never took his eyes off that bear's face. He feinted on the left, and then he feinted on the right, and then he moved in so quickly that some folks didn't see it happen, but my father did. He says that Ben feinted right in the middle, and when that bear grabbed, it looked as though his claws had grazed Ben's face, they were that much eye to eye, my grandpa and the bear. Then, before the bear could regain his balance, Grandpa had hugged him and thrown him to the ground.

"It was nothing," Ben said afterwards, dusting his hands off against his pants leg. "Just a question of timing, that's all." And the young bucks looked at old Ben Coffey with just a tad more respect.

Ben counted the carnival money in public, bill by bill, so folks could see that the carny people played fair. And his boys, June and Ray, "busted their buttons," or so my father says. "We must of been the proudest kids in Stamford that night."

Good thing Clara wasn't there to see him; she might have talked him out of it. She was a durn good sport, but she didn't have the spirit for taking a risk that Ben did, and her vegetable garden showed it. Her crops came in year after year, carefully tended and watered with water from the horse tank, while his . . . well, of course they didn't have irrigation then. With irrigation, things might have turned out different. Might have been, might have been. At least this year's gamble, on winter wheat, looked like it would pay off. The wheat stood tall and healthy in the sun; Ben had made arrangements with the same outfit that was combining his brother's land to take his crop. One day, maybe two more days to wait, then they'd gather the grain, take it to the elevator in town like gold to a bank. He was getting fidgety with waiting.

"Hey Stub," he hollered, and listened for a minute until he heard the three-legged pig's familiar grunt. Then Stub came limping around the corner of the barn, looking for a hand-out. Spoiled pig! He'd lost his leg in the fall, a couple of years ago, when Ben had been mowing the cane field. He'd thought he had all the pigs in—he had nearly two hundred head—but he'd missed this one, not that a red hog in a red cane field wasn't pretty easy to miss. The first thing Ben knew, the mower had scared the hog, and the dumb beast run right out in front of the sickle, caught his leg in it, and cut it off just below the knee. Ben had hollered at the boys to come and get him. "If you can save him, you can have him," he said. And the boys had taken the hog to the house. Clara got them alum water and silk thread; the boys pulled the pig's skin down over his stump, put alum water on it, and sewed the skin together over the stub end there. For a while, Ben thought they'd lose him, he just laid round the place, but Stub pulled through. Ben didn't put him back with the rest of the hogs but let him stay out as a pet—a promise is a promise—and every time anyone hauled feed corn out of the old header barge, to feed a horse or a cow or the hogs, why Stub would get some, too. He'd eat anything, that hog would. Ben remembered how tickled they all got one day when June fed him some fermented mash. Old Stub had guzzled down the whole bucketful like it was nothing, but when he tried to walk away, he couldn't. He was drunk. Ben laughed. There was nothing droller than a drunken three-legged pig trying to walk straight.

"We'll finish up this morning for sure," Ben's brother had said, but it was already noon and there was no combine in sight. Ben didn't like the look of the sky. Clouds rolling up from the south, the breeze cooler than it ought to be on a summer's day. Damn it all, he hoped they didn't get rained out on combining day.

"Come eat your dinner," Clara called, and he went in the house and dutifully shoveled food into his belly, but he couldn't keep his mind on the table. He kept listening, he didn't know for what. For the sound of the combine and the wagons coming up the road, he supposed.

When he heard it, a sort of pinging sound, he couldn't believe his ears. He stood up at the table so suddenly that his chair crashed behind him, and when Clara started, he said, "Shhhhh!" and cocked his ear. He could tell by the widening of her eyes that she had heard it, too. They headed toward the door. Ben pushed his way through first, just in time to see the storm burst overhead. Not rain but hail, big white pellets streaking down out of the sky. And wasn't it just his luck, he could see the combine coming down the road. There was a wagon ahead of it and a wagon behind it: the whole damn crew coming to reap a crop that wasn't going to be there for them to harvest.

When the hail let up, he walked out into his wheat fields. Well, he had survived the dust storms and the grasshopper plagues, so he supposed he could survive this, too, he thought, looking down at the broken stems under his feet. Hail! He stopped and lifted up one of the cold white balls. Big as a marble, hell, big as a taw, and for an instant he was transported to the boy he could have been, raised in the city, down on his knees, the taw resting on his index finger joint, his thumb itching behind. The chalk circle. The circle of talk over his head. The flick, the taw breaking the marbles: those hailstones had fallen thick as marbles on a sidewalk. Behind him, he could hear Clara weeping. Well, not weeping exactly, but breathing so high and thin it was as bad as weeping. Worse. Sounded like the high thin ping of those bastards as they'd hit the metal roof that was shielding the combine as it was being led in, god damn it to hail, he thought, and swallowed the choke in his own throat.

My dad always maintained that it was Ben's bad luck farming that killed him, and certainly my father's first act as a young man was to leave the farm behind him. Ben never recovered from the beating he took when that hail storm wiped him out of his whole wheat crop, Dad said, and certainly Ben did die young. He was only fifty-three. But the family story about his death is that he died laughing, laughing in his bed at some story he had heard. Maybe it was a new story, but I like to think it was a rehash of an old story that had become part of the family repertoire, like the time his son Tub got shot through with electricity and didn't even wince or the time June thought he'd surprise his father in the woods and he didn't know that Ben was cutting down a tree until he heard the "Timber!" and saw the old cottonwood coming right down his way. Ben could laugh until he cried, and would. He must have been doubled up like that when his heart gave way.

The Tornado

It was one of those hot, sticky days in May, at the height of the Great Plains' tornado season. The air was damp, the weather unsettled, the sky overcast. It must have been after four o'clock for I was already home from school, ensconced on the wooden platform that passed for a tree house in the huge elm that graced a corner of our back yard. I was reading, for the umpteenth time, *The Wizard of Oz*. "There came a great shriek from the wind," I read. "Then a strange thing happened. The house whirled around two or three times and rose slowly in the air. Dorothy felt as if she were going up in a balloon." The tornado that picked Dorothy up would carry her, I knew, from her home on the Kansas prairie to the Land of Oz. A strange occurrence indeed, but it didn't seem all that strange in Alma,

Picnickers watch a narrow tornado funnel, containing nature's fastest known winds, drop from a storm cloud. Courtesy Nebraska State Historical Society.

Nebraska, where I lived—on the fringe of Tornado Alley, that portion of the Great Plains that seems to spawn tornadoes. I'd heard stories—true ones—of a baby being plucked from his crib by a tornado and deposited unharmed on the ground, of a twister that wrenched the sheets off a bed but left the couple who'd been lying between them untouched, of the astonished farmer who watched a tornado remove the cow he'd been milking but leave him intact.

The back door slammed. I peered over the top of the book's pages in time to see my mother open the door to the screened-in back porch. "Marilyn," she called. "Margaret, Margery."

"I'm up here," I hollered down to her as we waited for my sisters to respond.

"Come down," she called. "The radio has tornado warnings out for Harlan County."

As I gathered together my few possessions, I turned and looked to the sky. In the southwest, where most tornadoes materialize, I could see a huge greenish-black thundercloud hanging on the horizon. Its underside was pendulous, clouds bulging downwards like grapes in a bunch. As I scrambled down the wooden steps my dad had nailed to the tree, I noticed that the breeze, which had been southerly a few minutes earlier, barely swaying the tips of the branches overhead, had stopped. An unaccountable stillness lay on the air, a silence as though a tornado had sucked up all the wind. No birds sang, no crickets chirped. Only my mother's strained voice could be heard—"Margaret! Margery!"—as I made my way to the back porch.

By the time we'd gathered up my sisters, we had no time to waste. "Quick," my mother said, "to the basement." And we made our way down the narrow wooden steps to the unfinished room that lay beneath our house, housing our washing machine and rinse tubs, and serving as shelter against any coming storm. If we'd had more time, we could have made our way across the alley to Grandma's storm cellar. We'd have been safer there among her canned peaches and pears. But as it was, we were happy enough to huddle—without being told—in the southwest corner of the basement, so that the twister, when it came spinning like a top and splintered the house into a thousand pieces, would blow the rubbish northeast over our heads.

Outdoors, the conditions were just right for forming a tornado. The cold air mass moving in from the Rocky Mountains had trapped beneath it a warm air mass moving up from the Gulf of Mexico. The warm air kept pushing its way up, looking for a weak point, a point of breakthrough in the cold air. By the time the warm air broke through, the horizontal winds were churning around it, beginning a vortex in the cumulonimbus cloud that caused the cloud to bulge. The swirling air mass began to push its way toward the ground. At first it was invisible. Then, as water in the humid air collected itself around the churning spiral, a gray cloud formed, a funnel that gradually lowered itself toward the earth from the massive green-black thundercloud that earlier had been moving in from the southwest. Had we been outdoors, we could have witnessed that rare phenomenon, the formation of a tornado cloud. Few eyewitness accounts describe such an event. One of them, by Milton Tabor, editor of the *Topeka Daily Capital* of Topeka, Kansas, describes the forming of a tornado in 1913: "The tornado formed where a group of students, including myself, were enjoying a picnic just east of Lincoln, Nebraska, and whirled furiously over our heads. We looked up into what appeared to be an enormous hollow cylinder, bright inside with lightning flashes, but black as blackest night all around. The noise was like ten million bees, plus a roar that beggars description." But we remained inside, content to cower behind the washtubs, intent on listening for a crackling of splinters that would mean the disintegration of the house over our heads, hearing nothing but the cracking static of the radio as the storm moved by.

Tornadoes occur all over the world, but nowhere more commonly than in the United States and, in the United States, nowhere more frequently or viciously than in the Great Plains area where the tornado season begins in the southern plains in February and moves gradually north as spring comes in. March, April, and May form the height of the tornado season on the plains. Nearly eighty percent of the twisters formed during the year occur in those three months, typically in the late afternoon or early evenings, although tornadoes have been known to form at any time of the night or day and in any month of the year. During the past half century, some 215 tornadoes occurred each year in the United States. These storms, although they do not threaten as wide an area as the hurricane, are much more devastating. They contain the fastest winds in nature. Speeds of up to two hundred miles per hour are not uncommon, and some scientists claim that tornadoes spin at speeds up to five hundred miles per hour. Just how fast a tornado spins has not been measured, for we lack instruments sturdy enough to survive the onslaught of the twister's winds. "A tornado is destructive," writes Louis J. Battan in *Natural History*, "because its power is concentrated in time and space." Tornadoes have been called the "little scourges of the air."

When the radio broadcast the all-clear signal, my mother, sisters, and I went back upstairs, relieved that the tornado, once again, had passed over our town. As the day progressed, however, reports drifted back that the twister had touched down at a farm house outside of nearby Ragan and, after supper, the family set out to see it. As we drove in toward the devastated farmyard, the first sight to catch our eyes — a sight that has stayed with me ever since — was that of a powerfully huge tree, much more enormous than the big elm that supported my tree platform in the back yard. It had been uprooted like a weed from a moist garden. It lay on its side, the tangled web of its enormous roots dangling helplessly in the air. The sight of the shattered farmhouse, the mangled farm machinery, was nothing compared to the realization that the storm that had so mercifully passed us by was capable of plucking that tree from deep inside the earth as though it were nothing but a carrot.

Several years later, my family and I were cruising along Highway 6 outside of Minden when my father spotted, off in the distance, a cloud with a long funnel hanging down from it, a funnel that looked like an elephant's snout, twisting and turning from side to side as it dipped toward the ground, turning from gray to black as it drew up dirt and debris from the earth. "A tornado," my father announced, somewhat grimly. "Looks like it's headed this way." And indeed it did. Moving in a southwest to northeast pattern, as tornadoes on the plains generally do, the funnel would be bearing down on us soon, or so it seemed. "Oh, Tom, what will we do?" cried my mother, although all of us knew the answer. A person in an automobile has only two choices when confronted with a twister: outdrive it or bail out of the car into the nearest ditch, grab both hands full of weeds, and pray. Both choices are chancy. Tornadoes can be outrun. They usually move at an average speed of 25 to 40 miles per hour, with the slowest being recorded at 5 miles per hour and the fastest at 139 miles per hour. They usually travel in a diagonal line, but some have been known to turn in circles or to U-turn and track back over their own paths. If this tornado weren't moving particularly fast, and if it stayed in its path, then we could probably outrun it. If. We would take our chances. The person praying in the highway ditch is counting on luck, too, for certainly few people in the open have directly confronted a tornado and lived to tell about it. Perhaps the tornado won't touch down in the ditch; perhaps it will pick up the car and leave the person behind. "Outrun it," my father decided, to no one's surprise. Terrified, we all hunkered down into the car to see whether my father's gamble would pay off this time. There was no question but that my father was a gambling man. He carried a silver dollar in his pocket for the purpose of matching his colleagues for a morning cup of coffee; he studied gin rummy texts at night so he could beat the odds at cards. Better to be taken trying to outrun the cloud than to calmly sit, like a fat pigeon, waiting to be taken — or so he must have figured. The auto picked up speed. We turned off Highway 6 to take a back road that, while it angled us closer to the storm, would let us shortcut our way out of its path. We watched the elephant's tail wobble in the sky. It seemed to grow larger, more ominous as we watched. The sight was similar to that recorded by R. V. Heidbreder when he spotted a Missouri tornado: "On looking toward the west a very much agitated cloud was seen. It was rolling and whirling for all it was worth. Then it seemed that a huge arm was slowly descending from the sky. It writhed and twisted about until it touched the ground. No sooner had it come into contact with the earth than it seemed to grow narrower until it looked like a slender ribbon." Or like that reported by Gayle Pickwell: "Unmistakable even to us who had never seen one before, the funnel cloud hung as a great thick rope in a long loose arch from the cloud above. Black at its upper end, it shaded out until the lower lengths were the color of escaping steam."

My father's bet paid off that day. We were successful in outrunning the funnel which crossed Highway 6 at some point behind our backs, leaving behind it who knows what kind of destruction. We never returned to find out.

In colonial days, those who witnessed tornadoes said that the noise they created sounded like the clatter of carriages rolling rapidly over rough cobblestone. When they touched down, they sounded like the explosion of cannon prolonged for a few minutes. In a more modern time, tornadoes are said to sound like a squadron of jets going overhead or like a train—hundreds of trains passing by or dozens of trains going through a tunnel. When high in the air, the tornado lets off a hissing, whistling noise—a screaming, hissing sound such as Dorothy heard when her tornado drew nearby. The shrill, high-pitched shriek may change to a terrible deafening roar as the tornado touches ground. When the tornado strikes, it sounds like a bomb exploding, witnesses say. This is probably due to the vacuum at the center of the funnel, a vacuum which causes wooden houses to literally explode into hundreds of fragments of timber. One woman, Mrs. Pearl Pruitt of Drumright, Oklahoma, described the sound of her house disintegrating around her as "like crackers being crushed in human hands."

Afterwards, the area in which a tornado has touched down

looks as though it had been bombed. Buildings are ripped open; houses are twisted on their foundations or missing altogether; cars, airplanes, and house trailers have been picked up, carried away, dropped, and smashed like toys. The vegetation is destroyed; small plants and shrubs are missing, leaving the earth barren, and trees are uprooted or broken off. One of the most disastrous of tornadoes in U.S. history was the one that hit Omaha, Nebraska, on Easter Sunday, March 23, 1913. Sunday had dawned as a balmy spring day, with glimpses of the sun becoming more fleeting until the threat of a storm developed into a full-fledged rainstorm out of which the tornado struck. The twister hit Omaha at 5:45 p.m., killing 139 and injuring 322. It passed through the residential section of the city, tearing up a path that averaged a quarter of a mile wide and five or six miles long. It moved from southwest to the northeast, in traditional fashion, passing through a wealthy section of town as well as through a poorer section. Fire broke out in twenty instances; a couple of hours passed before the fires were extinguished. Some 1,660 houses were damaged in the storm, leaving 2,179 people homeless. Six hundred forty-two of the houses were totally destroyed. Damage was estimated to be in excess of $8,000,000. "In the house, the sound was as of something ripping like canvas," wrote one eyewitness, "and eddies of power, not wind but electrical forces, grasped the buildings and sent them careening into a pile of twisted kindling or set them down with a jar in all kinds of grotesque poses. . . . The air was like sulfur and one felt as in a daze; no effort seemed intelligent, and those swift moments passed as a terrible nightmare. In an instant almost it was over. . . . Those ten seconds or more had left a trail of ruined homes and dazed, mangled, half-crazed victims. The demon had done its work and vanished again into the unseen."

"Half-crazed" victims are not uncommon after a tornado. Those who write of the tornado's aftermath speak of a "disaster syndrome," of dazed people staring blankly around them. The typical tornado victim is described as docile and cooperative, unlike victims of auto accidents who tend to be overwrought.

Omaha house collapsed from tornado suction during the Easter Sunday tornado of 1913, one of the most disastrous in the history of the United States. Courtesy Nebraska State Historical Society.

Perhaps the actual experience of one of these most violent of storms is a humbling experience. No matter how bad off you are, if you're alive, you know yourself to be in better shape than some of your neighbors.

The lightning that accompanies a tornado is "brighter, bluer, and more vicious than those of any other type of storm," writes Snowden D. Flora in his *Tornadoes of the United States*. Sometimes very bright sheet lightning is accompanied by interlaced lightning high in the clouds, lightning that creates a lace-like effect. At least one observer, Will Keller, a farmer near Greensburg, Kansas, who is one of the few people on earth who looked into the eye of a tornado and lived to tell about it, noted lightning at the center of the storm. He viewed the tornado from the doorway of his storm cellar, with the "great shaggy end of the funnel . . . directly overhead. Everything was as still as death. There was a strong gassy odor, and it seemed as though I could not breathe. There was a screaming, hissing sound coming directly from the end of the funnel. I looked up, and to my astonishment I saw right into the heart of the tornado. There was a circular opening in the center of the funnel, about fifty to one hundred feet in diameter and extending straight upward for a distance of at least a half a mile, as best I could judge under the circumstances. The walls of this opening were rotating clouds and the whole was brilliantly lighted with constant flashes of lightning, which zig-zagged from side to side." Many tornadoes exhibit active electrical activity with frequent flashes of lightning and, on occasion, funnels at night have been seen to glow as though lit from the inside. Indeed, the buzzing sound that sometimes accompanies a tornado, the sound that has been compared to the sound of a blowtorch, may be caused by small electrical discharges.

The storms spawn their share of freak occurrences, things like straws and stiff grass blades driven into the bark of trees or through fence posts or into the side of an old building. Timbers have been driven through animals and concrete roadways broken into fragments. The sudden lowering of air pressure can loosen the feathers of a chicken so it is plucked clean in an instant. A 1925 tornado carried a grain binder for a quarter of a mile, a pair of trousers for thirty-nine miles, and the lid of a compact for forty miles. A 1931 storm in Minnesota lifted up an 83-ton railroad coach with 117 passengers aboard and carried it eighty feet before dropping it in a ditch. Another railroad locomotive was spun 180 degrees and set down on the opposite track. One storm moved a crate of eggs five hundred yards without cracking one, while other tornadoes have hurled posts and large pieces of wood deep into the earth like javelins. The suction from another storm was strong enough to suck all the water from a well and to carry a cabinet full of dishes hundreds of yards, setting it down without a broken dish. And in June 1919, in Fergus Falls, Minnesota, in a storm that left fifty-nine dead, a car was captured in the crotch of a tree. The tree had been wrenched open by the twister and sprung shut again when released by the wind.

But the real fear of a tornado is the fear of being lifted bodily into the air and transported over great distances — à la Dorothy — only to be dashed to the earth or, as was the case with one woman plucked from her prairie home by a funnel, to be driven headfirst to the shoulders into the earth. On April 27, 1899, in Kirksville, Missouri, two women and a boy were picked up by a tornado which carried them over a church and set them back down on earth about a quarter of a mile away. Luckily, they were scarcely hurt. "I was conscious all the time I was flying through the air," one of the women reported, "and it seemed a long time. I seemed to be lifted up and whirled round and round, going up to a great height, at one time far above the church steeples. . . . As I was going through the air, being whirled about at the sport of the storm, I saw a horse soaring and rotating about with me. It was a white horse and had a harness on. By the way it kicked and struggled as it was hurled about I knew it was live. I prayed God that the horse might not come in contact with me, and it did not." The boy also saw the horse. It was directly over him in the vortex. He experienced the same fear of being kicked. Later, the horse was found, mud-plastered but uninjured a mile from town, and returned to its owner. It was considerably luckier than the herd of 160 panicked cattle that stampeded into a funnel near Apperson, Oklahoma, in 1935. All but five of them were found with their necks broken. Or the closely packed ranks of buffalo herds. Reports of tornadoes sweeping across the herds tell of the storms carrying individual animals weighing several tons through the air and dropping them, breaking nearly every bone in the animal's body when it was crashed to the ground.

Small wonder, then, that at the first warning of a tornado in the vicinity, people like my mother rounded up children and fled into the cellar for safety. Better to be standing in the basement of your own home, the walls coming down around your ears, than to be whirling overhead as though you were of no more significance than a speck of dirt or a drop of rain. And although a tornado had never touched down in Alma, where we lived—the funnel clouds would lift at the river bluffs south of town and leap over our little village—there was no trusting a tornado. Oklahoma City alone was struck twenty-six times by tornadoes in the eighty-year period following 1892, and the town of Codell, Kansas, was struck on the same date—May

20 — for three years in succession: 1916, 1917, and 1918. A storm could undo the work of a lifetime in an instant or two; it was nothing to argue with. You went into your shelter — as people in the Great Plains still do — and waited for that "upright, revolving, roaring, devastating cloud" to pass over, wondering what sort of a world you would be returning to.

The Great Lincoln Bank Robbery

No one could believe they were bandits, the nattily dressed, self-confident young men who stepped out of the blue Buick sedan with yellow wheels shortly after 10 a.m. They had the prosperous look and self-possession of businessmen—bankers, perhaps, coming to make an early morning deposit at the Lincoln National Bank and Trust Company in Lincoln, Nebraska. Elmer Beals, an old-time city patrolman, was standing across the street from the bank when the sedan pulled along the east side of the bank building, nestled next to the No Parking sign on Twelfth Street, and stopped, its engine running. He watched five men get out (a sixth man sat behind the wheel of the Buick). One

---

The Ganter Building, scene of the record-breaking Lincoln National Bank robbery in the 1930s. The bank lost so much money it closed its doors forever. Courtesy Nebraska State Historical Society.

man remained by the car, a second man, who held a Thompson submachine gun in his hand, stopped at the corner of the bank, and the three remaining men entered the bank. "It's just the sheriff's deputies guarding a money transfer," patrolman Beals told an inquisitive early morning shopper. "I saw them do the same thing last month during the Nebraska State Fair." And he continued on his rounds.

The day—Wednesday, September 17, 1930—had dawned hot and humid. At 10 a.m., a lazy sun was burning brightly through the haze as a smattering of early morning shoppers paused to window shop or made their way briskly down O Street, Lincoln's main drag. Allan McIntosh and Katherine Wilson were standing on the corner of Twelfth and O talking when a bandit with a machine gun ordered them to move on. Inside the bank, about twenty customers were patiently waiting for the tellers to open their cages and begin the transactions of the day. One teller, Edith Hult, was already taking care of a customer, Mrs. A. J. Anderson, when the bandits came walking through the door. Their movements were so businesslike and deliberate, their looks so respectable, their manner so poised that most people inside the bank thought it was a joke when one said, "Everybody down on the floor. This is a stickup." Not until the robbers began brandishing revolvers and pushing people around did it begin to dawn on customers and bank officials that this was, indeed, a holdup. Even so, none of them knew they were about to witness what would be for many years the biggest bank robbery in the history of the United States. Within eight minutes, the robbers would have cleaned the Lincoln National Bank and Trust Company out of $2,702,976 in cash and securities. Not long after that, they were gone, having vanished, as it were, into thin air. In less than ten minutes, a solid financial institution was rendered insolvent; two days after the robbery, the bank closed its doors, never to reopen again.

The movements of the robbers were deliberate and self-assured. They seemed to know the layout of the bank well. One of them paused behind the low railing that enclosed the teller cages and swung teller Phil Hall's chair around. "Get up," he ordered. Hall drew his fist back to strike the robber. Then he noticed the others. One of them struck Hall a blow on the head with his revolver butt, knocking him to the floor. The teller was stunned, but not seriously injured.

Teller Edith Hult first saw the bandits when one of them pushed her customer, Mrs. Anderson, aside and told them both to lie down. Mrs. Anderson dropped to the floor alongside other bank customers, but Miss Hult lay down inside the cage. This apparently displeased the bandit, who broke Miss Hult's small metal cage door, reached over, and struck her in the small of her back with the butt of his gun. "It was not a hard blow, but it caused some pain," Miss Hult said later. Figuring that the robber didn't want her inside the cage, the teller rose and joined the others lying on the main floor. The robber entered her cage and helped himself to the cash, leaving behind the silver.

While one bandit scooped up cash from the tellers' cages and deposited it in a bag, and another bandit guarded the officers and customers, the third bandit went to the basement and commanded four bookkeepers who were working there to come upstairs and lie on the floor with the others. Then, led by teller Hall, he went to the rear of the bank where the vaults were located. The robbers called out for assistant cashier H. E. Leinberger, who knew the combination to one of the vaults, but he was not there. He had gone on an errand to the state house. When the bandits determined that Leinberger was gone, they called out for someone to open the safe, and assistant trust officer Florence Zeiser, who knew the combination to one safe, got up off the floor. What happened next is not exactly clear. One account says only that the bandit "then forced Miss Zeiser to open the vault." Another account says that after Miss Zeiser had opened one vault, the bandits told her to open the other. She said she didn't know the combination. The bandit then said, "Well, shoot her."

Frightened, Miss Zeiser screamed, "I said I cannot do it!"

The bandit motioned with his gun. "Go on over and lie down," he said, and that vault was never opened.

A third account maintains that the thieves got the securities in the vault entirely by chance. The paper was in a heavy safe protected by a time lock. When bank vice-president E. H. Luikart ordered a teller to show the gunman that the safe could not be opened, to everyone's surprise the door swung open and the bandits stuffed bonds into a woolen blanket that one gunman had carried under his arm into the bank. That morning someone had forgotten to set the time lock.

Outside the bank, a young man, W. W. Hill, stood staring at the picture of the University of Nebraska football team in the bank window when he felt someone seize him by the wrist. "Someone wants to see you inside," he was told, and Hill looked up to face a tall, good-looking young man dressed nattily in a brown tweed suit. Thinking that there had been some mistake, Hill said that he wasn't wanted anywhere, but he changed his mind when the gunman brandished his weapon. "Oh, yes you are," the gunman said, and dragged a reluctant Hill into the bank and onto the floor.

About that time, a Mrs. Hugh Werner stepped into the bank and understood instantly that a robbery was underway. She slipped back outside, walked east across Twelfth Street to the Crancer Music Store and told the storekeeper, E. S. Wolfenbarger, that a robbery was in progress across the street. Wolfenbarger called the police, but his message wasn't too clear. "Something's going on at Twelfth and O Streets," he said, but he didn't say what. Curious himself, and thinking that by now the bandits would have had time to escape, Wolfenbarger walked over to the bank. He was on the point of telling the bandit holding the submachine gun — whom he mistook for a bank official (he had a pencil over one ear) — that he had called the police when the bandit jabbed the gun into his stomach, cutting his words short. The bandit forced Wolfenbarger into the bank where he took his place on the floor along with the other customers.

At police headquarters, some four or five blocks away, detective Peter Meyer and motor officer Schappaugh got into a cruiser to go investigate Wolfenbarger's complaint. They expected to find an early-morning drunk carrying on. When they parked, the robber's lookout walked over to them, pointed the submachine gun at them, and said, "Get that police car moving or you're dead." The pair reluctantly pulled away, then sped back to police headquarters to get help.

Dr. Earl C. Alldritt was in the Ben Wolf Cigar and News store at 121 North Twelfth Street when a customer walked in and announced that a man with a machine gun was standing on the corner. "Must be making a movie," the two men decided. Then Dr. Alldritt went on down the street to investigate. He was met by a husky individual who ordered him inside the bank, emphasizing his words with his gun. Dr. Alldritt lay down on the floor just in time to watch a robber walk by with a bag of loot. "All right, Jack, let's go," one robber said, and they headed out the door, carrying a bag full of money and a red and yellow plaid blanket full of securities.

W. E. Barkley, president of Lincoln Joint Stock Land Bank and the largest stockholder in the Lincoln National Bank and Trust Company, walked into the bank just as the robbers were leaving. He got slugged on the head with a revolver butt, a blow that badly gashed open the right side of his head. Two men helped him to Dr. Earl N. Deppen's office, where four stitches were taken to close the wound.

As the robbers left the bank, one of them said to another, "Well, that's another good job well done." The robbers walked out with the money — $35,000 in cash and more than $2.5 million in securities, including valuable Liberty Bonds that couldn't be replaced — in so leisurely a fashion that Alfred Beckman, who saw them leave, thought the bank was sending money to some other bank in town. They got into the car in an orderly manner; apparently their seating had been prearranged. The lookout with the machine gun was the last to get into the car. Then the robbers turned on a siren and headed down Twelfth Street.

By this time, the police — alerted by officers Meyer and Schappaugh — had returned to the bank. They followed the speeding car south on Twelfth Street. The bandits tried to turn east on N but had to continue in order to avoid a collision. They turned east on L, silencing the siren as they turned, and disappeared south on Thirteenth Street. The police, at this time just a notch above being night watchmen, lost the getaway car as it wove a path through the southeast section of the city and went on into the open country. The use of a siren was a master touch; it cleared a path for the robbers. Motorists and pedestrians moved out of the way, thinking that the getaway car was a police or fire vehicle. Deputy Sheriff Cecil Strawn, who was driving west on O Street, heard the siren and saw the car; he thought it was a police car. F. D. Throop, publisher of the *Lincoln Star*, saw the car as it roared past the Star building.

Back at the bank, the word of the robbery spread slowly, but as it spread, a crowd began to gather. The crowd jammed the bank so that it was difficult for the officers to get the information about the robbery that they needed. Pictures show the crowd thronging around the corner of Twelfth and O, where it stayed for hours after the robbery.

Police began to get contradictory descriptions of the robbers, and conflicting reports from people who said they had sighted the getaway car. The police theory was that the bandits had headed for Kansas City over the back roads, but farmer Frank Backman, near the western outskirts of Omaha, reported to police that a blue Buick sedan with Iowa plates had sped by his farm at a high rate of speed, then stopped in front of his house to change a tire. "There were five men in the car, and they all seemed very nervous," Backman said. "One of them said to me, 'Will you help get this damn car going again? We're in a hell of a hurry. We've got to catch a train.' " The farmer saw several objects in the car, including one that looked like a submachine gun. Two shotguns lay in the back. "They changed the tire and went on north, driving very fast," stated Backman.

Reports of stolen private planes led law officials to speculate that the robbers had made a getaway by air, but a day later, a young boy confessed to having stolen the planes for a lark. Some lawmen still believe that the bandits had a moving van parked on a side road outside of Lincoln. According to them, the robbers drove the car up a ramp, closed the back doors, and slowly ambled toward Kansas City, Missouri, where Johnny Lazia, a politician and ex-con, offered them protection—for a big price. The license plate, Iowa 97-13557, was traced to a Chevrolet belonging to Howard Sween of Sioux City. The plates had been stolen two months before.

No one knew how big the robbery was at first because bank officials tended to play down the loss. Initially officials said that a large amount of securities had been overlooked by the robbers, and that the loss was fully covered by insurance. Then, two days after the robbery, the bank closed its doors, never to reopen them.

Six months after the robbery, the lawmen still didn't have any solid leads. "I can't even call the FBI," complained county attorney Max Towle. "Someday they will make bank robbery a federal offense and we can get the help of the FBI." Today, of course, they could have.

Thomas O'Connor of East St. Louis, Illinois, was arrested in May 1931 as a suspect. Police raided his apartment. They found him with Jack Britt, Howard Lee, Tommy Hayes, Edward O'Hara, and William McQuillin. Witnesses from Lincoln identified O'Connor, Britt, and Lee as gang members. On May 18, 1931, the three were brought from Chicago to Lincoln on a special railroad car on Burlington's Ak-Sar-Ben Limited. "We don't have anything to worry about," Britt maintained. "That damned county attorney Towle doesn't have any good case against us." But he was wrong. After several stormy court sessions, O'Connor and Lee were convicted. They were sentenced to twenty-five years in the Nebraska State Penitentiary. Britt, however, was acquitted after two Lincoln juries deadlocked during spectacular trials. The turning point in Britt's trials came when a convict and key state witness, George Stoy, confessed that he had lied in the three cases in the hopes that the publicity would serve to spring him from prison. Surprisingly, despite legal maneuvers by their Lincoln lawyers, O'Connor and Lee were never granted new trials. They served for ten years, being pardoned in September 1941 for crimes they both strongly denied. Both left the state and neither sued Nebraska for imprisoning them or for any aspect of their arrests or famous trials.

Gus Winkler, a close friend of Chicago gangster Al Capone, was also charged late in 1931 with the holdup. The onetime boss of Chicago's northside rackets argued that he had been in Buffalo, New York, on an assignment for Capone on the day the robbery occurred. But he was afraid that this alibi might not stand up in Lincoln's "hick courts."

"I'll get back the missing securities if you drop the robbery charges against me," said Winkler. "But I have to get back to Chicago."

Towle wasn't about to make the decision to dismiss Winkler lightly. He conferred with high-ranking governmental officials, including Nebraska governor Charles Bryan; he discussed the matter with bank officials and others. At stake was the financial life of some prominent Lincoln families who faced financial ruin unless at least some of the stolen Liberty Bonds were returned. Finally, after much consideration, Towle dropped the charges.

"The whole affair is one of the blackest pages in Nebraska history," said Governor Bryan when he heard of Towle's decision.

Winkler was good to his word. Early in January, 1932, Chicago police received an anonymous phone call. "Go to the corner of Armitage and Newcastle at 2 a.m.," the caller said. "You'll find the securities under the lamp post." Detectives found a suitcase bulging with $583,000 in stolen Liberty Bonds plus an affidavit stating that $2 million more had been burned.

Winkler's body was later found in Chicago with 111 shotgun slugs in it. Underworld circles maintained that his connection with the Lincoln bank robbery was responsible for his gangland slaying.

Towle continued to work on the case but, at his retirement in 1947, he left it behind with no major developments.

Years later, the FBI in the course of solving other national crimes believed they learned who actually robbed the bank. Their list included Homer Wilson, a Chicago gangster who was supposedly the gang's leader; Edward (Willy) Bentz, once a member of the famous Machine Gun Kelly gang with a long criminal record including bank robbery; Charles Joseph Fitzgerald, a participant in the Hamm kidnapping at St. Paul, Minnesota; Cas Stone, a minor underworld figure; Avery Simons, a rancher in Bolivia following the Lincoln crime; and Eddie Doll (alias Eddie LaRue), an Iowan linked with the stolen Liberty Bonds. None of these men was ever prosecuted for his part in the Lincoln crime.

PART III

Water

My Flood Story

by Arlene Dake Mintzmyer
as told to Marilyn Coffey

Woodman, spare that tree!
Touch not a single bough!
In youth it sheltered me,
And I'll protect it now.

It was the 31st of May, 1935, and I was in my folks' house northwest of Orleans, Nebraska, with my father, Alvin C. Dake, who was about forty-nine at that time, and my mother, Minnie E. Dake, forty-eight, who was a Schwabauer before she was married. I was nineteen years old. We'd had lots of rain and we knew the water was coming up, but our phones had gone out, so we didn't get any phone warning. Communications were so much vaguer in those days, but we always heard when water was high up the river.

My two brothers, Clarence, twenty-four, and Gerald, twenty-two, were not in the house at this time. We had an old flat-bottom boat that the boys and Dad made; it was metal outside and wooden lined, and when the boys saw the water

---

An edited transcript of a taped interview.

Arlene Dake Mintzmyer's high school graduation picture, taken about a year before the Republican River flood swept her downriver. She was the last survivor rescued. Courtesy Arlene Dake Mintzmyer.

coming up in our pasture, they had taken this boat and gone way down in the timber toward the river where they had saw logs — walnut logs — which they used to make furniture. They'd taken the logs to a sawmill and made cedar chests in manual training and a lot of furniture for their own sake. In fact, my brother Clarence had just finished a beautiful bedroom outfit, a bed and a vanity. They went down to chain the logs to other trees so they wouldn't float away. The afternoon before the flood, we got word of higher water coming. My dad took a team and wagon and went down and got our neighbors, the Neumeyer family, George Henry ("Hank") Neumeyer, and his wife, Irene, and their little girl, Dorothy, five years old (I remember she was telling me that evening how she was going to start school that fall), and their little boy, Bobby, three. Their house was closer to the river than our house which was west of the river about a mile or so, so Dad had gone around and got these folks. At the supper table that evening, my dad told the little neighbor girl, "I had a dream last night that I was rescuing a little girl from flood waters. Do you suppose that was you?" As I look back on that incident, I believe most strongly in premonition.

After the children were put to bed and the grown-ups were getting ready to retire, we were awarded by a severe wind and rain storm. Rain and hail and everything. Anxiety was great for the return of the boys. Dad and Mr. Neumeyer took a kerosene lantern and went down to the barn to keep vigil — to watch for the boys, and to turn the horses out into a lot. My father had — I'm not quite qualified to say — probably twelve or fourteen horses, at least that many. The men was down at the barn quite a while. As the storm grew worse, they decided to come to the house and were met by a wall of water. The water was waist deep on them; they barely made it to the porch and into the house.

Our house was a newer house, only three or four years old, and it was up on blocks quite a ways, but almost immediately water began to come up from the basement through the furnace registers (the ones with seats on them and the air comes out the side). Then it began to pour through the windows, and the boys still weren't back. Unknown to us, they were in the boat when the flood hit, and it took them way across the river and just rolled them. After, they said that miraculously one of them got up in a tree and he looked and the other one was in the same tree. Now when a storm came, we usually went down cellar—a storm cellar. Dad had finished it, put cement all over the thing. But we didn't have the time. Had we of done that, well, that cave was swept out. It would just have been a tomb, that's all. Ours was a two-story house, so the women and kids went up to the second floor, and we began carrying things upstairs, hoping we could save them. I remember we took box after box of chickens and ducks and turkeys upstairs into the east bedroom, and we took some things out of the china closet. On one of the last trips downstairs, I picked up my class ring (Orleans High School, 1934) and put it on, thinking that it might be a means of identification. About that time we was wading barefooted way deep in water and my mother said, "Dear," she said, "I wish you wouldn't go down there any more." So I had come up and, beings I stopped, the men did, and we was just standing there near the top of the stairs when the sides of the stairway all went together and a great big log came right through.

About this time the house kind of wrenched or tipped or something, and the water wasn't so deep in the west bedroom so we went over there. Dad saw a baseboard was wrenched loose, so he took it and broke the window out; it was kind of a small upstairs window. He crawled out and got his arm up in this bracket thing and began getting people out of the window and up on the roof. My mother went out first and my dad had her what he thought was safely on the roof, and I remember looking at the alarm clock on the boys' dresser; it said twenty minutes of four. I noticed that the chickens and ducks and turkeys in the east room were silent; I think they must have drowned. And Mr. Neumeyer was on the bed with the little boy in one arm and a kerosene light at that time in the other. The mother was just naturally quite frantic. I'd given the little girl my big baby doll which was wearing my baby clothes—especially do I remember what that doll had on, one of those little curly coats, fake fur we'd call it now—and Dorothy was clinging to that doll as if it were her mother. I said to Mr. Neumeyer, "You take your family out, and I can go out, and you can come out," and he didn't say anything. Finally he said, "No, we're taking our chance inside." I waited obviously as long as I could, until everything was floating toward the window, and those cedar chests that the boys made got so deep in the water they just flipped and started out, and the lids would come open, and everything was going for the window. We had a collie dog named Mac who had never been in the house before. Sensing danger, he had pushed himself into the house when the men came back from the barn. Now he wanted to get out the window before I got there, and the water was even with the sill, and I'll never forget pushing things back to get out the window. I was fighting to get out, too. That's where I got this glass in my hand. And as I came out that window, I remember my mother, she spoke to me and she said, "Arlene, are you there?" I assured her I was. The dog went out before me, and I was just coming out. Dad grabbed me—we had ahold of hands—and about that time, everything crashed.

I was plunged into ice-cold water. Now you must remember that all was darkness; it was raining, and the water was roaring so, you couldn't hear yourself or anybody else speak hardly. Later, people that was on the outside of the flood tell you that it roared so you couldn't hear, so you can imagine what it would be inside of it. It would really be something. People ask me so many times if I was a swimmer. I wasn't very much at swimming—at that time I was trying to learn—but I had a knowledge of what to do when I was pulled under the water. I had played in the river a lot. As kids, we took the boat up the river and would float down. The river was our swimming pool in those days, and thank goodness I knew water. I never had a fear of it. I think if I'd of had a fear of water, I wouldn't have been here. But my greatest asset, I think, was to have a calm disposition.

My father had ahold of me when the house crashed, and then we went our separate ways; afterwards he mentioned that one time when he came up he remembers getting ahold of somebody, and I think I did kind of have ahold of somebody there. I

The Republican River flood of 1935 swamped many a small town nestled near its banks, such as this one. Courtesy Nebraska State Historical Society.

fought to get away because I was just fighting to keep myself going, you know. The water was thick with stuff, timber and boards and debris, and I got hit by things. I often said that I'd get between boards, and I'd just roll right through them. That's the truth. I was black and blue, and nail holes were all over my body. You could see the water swirling, and you'd get in that, and it would pull you down. In the deepest water, there would be whirlpools, great giant whirlpools that would suck you down just like a suction, and it was all darkness. Well, like I said, I was just a-fighting and a-struggling and trying to hold my breath long enough to get a gasp of air. If I grabbed something, I went a little ways with it. My father said that he grabbed onto a piece of wreckage and hung on; therefore, he crossed that river—what *was* the river, *everything* was a river at that time. The old Indians said bluff to bluff, and this is true; the water ran from bluff to bluff. But my dad crossed the old river, and he got so much further than me. I went down and hit the timber, but he just went on. I went into the timber quite a ways—I fought around a little bit to get in through there—just grab on and go as I could. I tried to stay kind of on myself, so I didn't go far. I didn't quite get to the river channel. Then I come up against a fairly big tree and put my arms and legs around it and clung to it. I was neck-deep in water and, like I said, there was such a terrific roar you wouldn't hear anything and such darkness you couldn't see anything, and it wasn't so much to me only to keep fighting stuff away, to keep pushing stuff away, because the debris, too, was coming right through the timber. I have often said that these boards that would come down, they were pliable, more like a rag than a board, and they would just get around you and just scrape and grate you.

I stayed in the first tree until daylight. And all the time before daylight, I had thought I hadn't gone very far. I thought I was in our yard—we had some great big cottonwoods in our yard—but when it begin getting light enough that I could detect where I was, I realized I sure wasn't in our yard. The tree I had ahold of was tall and had no branches close enough to reach, but not too far away was another tree with a crotch a ways above the water. I'm not a tree climber, either, but I climbed my tree and there was a grapevine, and I steadied myself with the grapevine and got up in those other trees and stayed there. I was riding high—I wouldn't be surprised if maybe I was ten feet above the ground. When I was sitting high in this second tree, I could touch my feet to the water. I still didn't know where I was. There was mostly water in every direction as far as I could see. A lot of people say, "The river, was it up this far or that far?" and I say, "Well, I wouldn't know. I was right in the middle." I thought I was the lone one, but unknown to me, my brothers were safe across the river channel, on the east side, and when it became daylight, they searched around a little and found their boat. Some planes went over, and the boys had the idea that the planes were looking for them two. They were not thinking that we would be gone by any means; they thought our place was too far from the river. So they were thinking they were the only ones lost, and I was thinking I was the only person alive.

It was better in the second tree. The water was brownish-red, and it was thick with dirt from the dust storms and all things like that, and tumbling all over itself. There was so much debris everywhere, thrashing through the water. Stuff would be flopping and twisting and crashing and so on, all the time.

Sometimes a big tree would be coming down through the timber standing straight up, and all your lumber and stuff, it would just upend and go every way. Many's the time I watched a tree come bolting toward my tree, and I thought it would bump it and knock it over, but it would just hit my tree and bounce. Then later there were some planks and stuff wedged between those trees, and we had a pet colt, Janey, we had raised up on the bucket. She was always getting into something. Mom would put out the chicken feed and Janey'd run right through the chickens to get attention. I remember that spring; the men were painting our house (it was a bungalow), and in those days, you mixed your own paint with a white paint made out of lead. Well, Janey saw that white paint in the can, and she thought it was milk, and we had to get the vet to save her. I remember the night before the flood, Dad was breaking her—she was a couple of years old then, a great big sorrel—and he had her harnessed with some other horses. When the team came into the yard, the other horses'd go to the tank to drink, but here she'd come into the barn with her harness and all still on to have her milk out of the bucket. Well, she had drowned with the flood and come down and lodged right under my tree for a while.

One thing I remember: I had a dress and a slip on, and there was just a great big tear right out of the front, so on Saturday, I took my slip off and reversed it. And then one time I heard a plane go over and I took my dress off and I just waved. It was a pink dress that I'd made; I made all my own clothes. A piece of that dress is in a quilt I have. Of course, the people in the plane didn't see me or anything. But that was the only chance I thought I had. I would make the remark, too, that when my brothers were coming back through with the boat, they had come, well, I wouldn't say close, but they had come not too awful far from where I was in that tree. They worked their way across on Saturday afternoon. The boat didn't have any oars left, but the boys got lumber and such and used it as their paddles and their means of getting back across the river. Like I said, they had no idea when they got out that we were gone. People told them. And they could see that our place and everything was missing. Such a jolt. Then they say it wasn't too much after that Dad came out. He came out just north of the Silverway Bridge, the railway bridge which was two miles west of Orleans. He said he kind of hung on to this little sapling tree, and on Saturday he worked himself from tree to tree and got up on this grade and yelled and people finally came down and helped him get up. So the boys more or less searched around for Mom and me until dark and they had to give it up.

I couldn't quite figure out where I was at because I was way up high. Well, on Saturday sometime during the day, I could look down and see a rock wall. I recognized that as being our neighbor's; their house was kind of up and they had a brick wall on each side of it. Therefore I kind of got my bearings where I was at. I had visions of several places that I was until I located that very place. Then I knew I'd come, well, approximately a mile and a half, I think maybe. It had gotten cloudy and was pretty cold in there above the ice water, I guess, and I had wounds in my hands from the glass and the nails. Every once in a while, the sun would shine through, and I would hold my hands up. You couldn't imagine the comfort and the warmth of the sun on my wounds. Then toward evening, about dusk, I looked over in the water and I thought I saw a person, possibly with their head back, and I knew they had red hair. Well, coincidentally, the neighbors that were with us had red hair, and I just . . . It was sort of a mirage everywhere, and I don't know what; I couldn't see too plain. I always thought it was a person. Well, I watched that until way in the night, just the motion of it. Not too far from where I was there was a great big hill. They say that folks built big bonfires and stayed on the shore and watched all night, but I didn't see the fires. One time, way in the night, somebody turned a car light on; well, I was pretty sure it was a car light, and I thought, "Well, then there's life, I guess." You got to feeling you were pretty much the only one, anymore; I thought I was the only existing person. I didn't sleep. All night long there was a crash and a slam and a bang, and I was afraid of something hitting my tree. I watched that thing in the water all night long. It just seemed to ride the waves, you know, up and down, and you didn't want to believe, and yet you wondered, all the time, what it was. By morning it had raised up and I could see that it was a horse—more or less the tail part, you know. It looked like a person's head.

After over thirty hours of sitting in the crotch of the tree, I climbed down Sunday morning with the idea of working my way out of the timber, as I felt all my family was gone. I was just so stiff and all, from nail holes and everything, hands and legs and all. I was just scratched to pieces, and paralyzed, but I made up my mind and, after it got light quite a while, I got down out of that tree and stood on the great piles of debris beneath it. My legs and hands were swollen stiff. While wondering what I might do, I heard this pounding. I couldn't see anything through the branches much, and then I got the idea that when they quit pounding, I was going to yell. I did that several times, and they started pounding again. It was a long time before they began coming. I could see some figures and they came, and as the boat and men became visible I was most happy and surprised to recognize it as my brothers and another man, Edward E. Johnson. He was a country surveyor at that time, but he lived over on the Sappa. They were pounding the boat together where it had been wrecked so they could come in and search. Some of them had heard somebody yell. They knew somebody was in there alive. I was so surprised when I saw that it was my brothers. I thought all of the family was gone; we had given the boys up as lost when the water took our house. Nobody could tear you apart inside worse than I was, but we didn't say much. One of the first things they asked me was, "Who else is here?" I said, "There isn't, and there hasn't been." They told me that Dad was waiting at the water's edge. Only silence assured me that our mother had not been found.

To get the boat out, my brothers and Ed would swim to a tree and pull the boat and swim to another tree and pull the boat. After they got me out of the timber, the current was so strong that folks waded in with great big old hay ropes from the other side, and they caught our boat as we went by. As our boat got closer and I could see so many people, I suddenly had the urge not to go ashore. If I could have jumped back in, I would have. But the sight of my father so anxiously waiting to see who was being rescued soon made me want to get to his waiting arms. I got in a lumber wagon and was transported from the field to a road and a waiting car, to be driven to Stamford to see the family doctor, Dr. J. N. Campbell. He had been the doctor when I was born nineteen years before. About that time word got around that they had found somebody. And would you believe it, they blocked the roads and everything? People were coming and coming and you couldn't get through, hardly. And one neighbor, an old fellow, he had his car and he took Dad and I to Stamford. Well, Dr. Campbell wasn't in his office. He was out of town taking care of a sick lady—doctors went to the homes in those days—and she had pneumonia. The doctor heard I was found so he rushed into town and—I'll never forget—he come out into the street; I didn't get out of the car, and the main thing he give me was whiskey. Then they took me to this neighbor's place, Ben Peterson's place, and put me to bed and washed me and bathed me and just about covered me with Merthiolate for all the scratches. In the afternoon, the doctor came around again, and he decided that I had double pneumonia and everything else. Then he sent in and got typhoid shots, so I was very close to having typhoid.

That first night a neighbor lady, Mrs. Lillian Hasenyager, slept with me, and when they put me in bed, they had my covers so tight that I couldn't move. When the moon came out, I woke and looked out the window and saw the moon shining on the new washed-in sand. I thought it was water coming up. I woke Mrs. Hasenyager up. "You better get out of here," I said. "I can't move, but you better get out." I guess she thought I was delirious. And after that night, I didn't have a fear of water, but I had a fear of, well, claustrophobia, you might say. To this day I can't tolerate tight places.

And I'll never forget the afternoon that somebody came to see me and they opened the door, and Mac, our collie dog, rushed in and under the bed. They had to drag him out. But he knew. He came to the water's edge on Saturday; they found him and they knew whose dog he was. He was just overwhelmed with joy to see my dad and brothers. Now you wouldn't think a dog could get out, but he did. He got out someway. We don't know.

My mother and the four neighbors were still missing. The boys immediately resumed the search, leaving each morning to search and returning each evening. Well, people misconstrue things pretty badly. My brothers and Ed knew there were two distinct voices where they found me, and that really put them on the wrong track. After they got me ashore, why, they went right back in there searching, but they never found anybody. Well, there never had been two voices. On Tuesday evening, my brothers told me that they had found our mother's body. They wouldn't say too much about it. It's undescribable, I would imagine. Funeral arrangements were made for Friday at the Orleans Methodist Church. Orleans was on the other side of the river, only a few miles away, but the bridges were all out, so Thursday I was taken around Alma way. The Alma bridge was open to foot traffic, so I was carried across the river there on a stretcher and taken to friends' home in Orleans. It was about a 35-mile trip around the river. Our family stayed with these friends, Mr. and Mrs. William Porter, for almost a month. Clothes were borrowed and given to us for the funeral. Friday morning I realized I was too sick to attend services. I was real bad that day, so I couldn't go. The church ladies served a nice dinner and sent food to the house. That p.m. I was taken to Oxford, to Dr. F. W. Shank, since travel back to see Dr. Campbell was about impossible. My legs had turned black from blood poisoning — the poisoning was way above my knees — and I was just perforated with nail holes, some of them so big I could stick my whole finger in them. Dr. Shank looked at my legs and he said, "I never knew a person could be alive with legs like that." He thought the poisoning was impossible to treat, so he called in two different doctors to see. Amputation was thought best. He told me that my legs would probably have to be amputated, but nevertheless he lanced my feet. He slit the side of each foot, and when he did, pus and little bits of sticks and everything poured out of them. He let me go back to be with Dad because pretty much we were a broken family. And there was a kind neighbor lady in Orleans that helped me, a practical nurse, I would say, a real motherly nurse. She come and soaked my feet and took care of all my wounds for a long time. I didn't lose my legs—I was too tough—but the nerves, they never recovered. It's just numbness. And I still have glass in my hand where I grabbed the window, you see. There's no way of getting the glass out. A cyst forms around it. And after about a week or so, I broke out all over with poison ivy, every place. They said the water was full of it. I'm immune to it now. And I remember the boys, Clarence especially, coming in from searching, and he would bathe my legs and press the pus out. I remembered my mother's last words: "Arlene, are you there?" They were definitely her last words. And I remembered the doll that Dorothy Neumeyer was clinging to, and I always said, if they found my dolly, they'd find the little girl. I was told they found parts of what they thought was my doll, but the little girl has never been found. They found the little boy and the mother and the father; my brothers found the father's body. And another woman's body was found later, in a silo; they had washed down the river together. I was listed in the newspaper as dead, so they got a telegram off to my Grandmother Schwabauer in California, but it was days before she got that telegram. She got a letter from me about the same day—the mail was very prompt in those days—and they said that was the most joyous time in their lives, even though they'd lost my mother, of course, to know that I was alive, to hear from me.

We lost nearly everything. Our place was leveled, and our pond and our basement was filled in with dirt. Now at that time we had CCC boys. They were young fellows without a job and the government hired them. We had a lot of respect for the CCC boys. They did a lot of dirty work, burying dead animals and going through all the debris. My dad took treats to them. I certainly would give them credit for coming out and doing a lot of cleaning up. The CCC boys dug out our basement. We had a ledge around it, and they dug some fruit out of it, would you believe it. And we salvaged a tractor—a Caterpillar—out of the pond. We found Clarence's new 1935 Ford, and the family car, and my little '29 Ford Coupe. We had to tear out all the upholstery, the sand had packed behind it, and behind the dashboard. All the mechanisms, your meter and your gauges and so on, were packed with sand, but we salvaged the cars. And about a mile and a half down the river, we found a piece of the house stuck in the trees. We think it floated down the river until it struck trees and crushed like an egg shell.

Lots of our things we never found. We couldn't find the piano, or our tractors (we lost a Fordson tractor, an all-steel tractor). The water was just a whirling thing; it would dig a hole and then maybe a piece of heavy machinery would drop into that hole, and it would catch the dirt and fill over it. And for years after, the men would see a lever or something, and they'd dig it out, and it would be quite a sizeable piece of machinery. One time they did dig out a corn binder, and under it was a quart jar of canned apples, and it was some yellow apples that my mother and I had canned. We just had the flats on the jars, and would you believe that jar was sealed? And they found a trunk, and it was partly smashed, but these six custard glass goblets were in there. It was part of a lemonade set that was a wedding present of my folks from Lake Prior near Woonsocket, South Dakota, where they were married in 1907. And within the next year, my dad found the pitcher for the set buried halfway in the sand. The rose on one side is all bleached off from facing the sun, and at one time the pitcher had a watermark along it. They found a quilt that my mother made hanging in a tree, and a doll's cup from my tea set where they were plowing, and one of our feather pillows floated six or seven miles and got inside Jim Ralston's screened-in porch. I have the pillowcase yet, made out of a feed sack. I had embroidered a little Dutch boy and appliquéd the pants part.

The Red Cross did help us build a small house out there, and we supplemented a great deal. As far as furnishings, I know a lot of people did get them through the Red Cross, but ours mainly came from friends and relatives. We didn't need everything in those days, you know. It was a rough hard life, trying to get going again. You can imagine how it would be.

The next fall, after the flood, we took my Grandmother Schwabauer to visit her son, he's a minister at Benkleman, and south of Benkleman we saw this tree which was buried upside down by the flood water. And we went out, after the flood, and took a picture of my father standing by his little sapling tree, and a picture of me and my trees, and I said, "This is the first one I come up against." Later I was going to carve on that tree, "Woodman, spare that tree. In flood it cradled me, and I hope to protect it now," but I never did. I'm not sure I would recognize the tree now, I haven't been down there in so long.

Isn't it strange how things happen? I took Normal Training in high school, but I was home that year before the flood, and my mother and I, we had a wonderful time that year. Now people will make the remark, "I suppose you don't like to see things or hear things that remind you." Well, I'm not that kind of a person because there's nothing but what reminds you of a thing like that in your life. You think about it all the time as far as that goes. You could lose all of your possessions, which would be nothing when you've lost a life such as your mother's. And people will say, "Do you hate to hear about it?" Well, definitely. Especially this time of the year, around June 1st.

The Republican River Flood

When folks in south-central Nebraska, where I was born and raised, speak of The Flood in tones of deferential awe, they may mean the flood that set Noah's ark to rest on Mount Ararat, but more likely they are referring to the Republican River Valley flood of 1935. As a child, I was hard-pressed to know which was the more impressive. Noah's flood, it's true, covered the entire universe with maybe only a couple of mountaintops left sticking up, but it was a slow flood, lasting more than a year. Nothing was slow about the Republican River flood. It came, said those who had seen it, like a wall of water, some eight to ten feet high, a churning wall that could turn a windmill in its path as easily as though it were a toothpick, a roaring wall that sounded like a freight train passing through. In less than two days, it had

The Nebraska Light & Power Company building as it looked before the Republican River flood of 1935. Courtesy Nebraska State Historical Society.

flooded the entire river valley, from its beginnings in Colorado to its joining of the Kansas River in Kansas. En route, it killed more than a hundred people.

Some days, when I was feeling pious, I would daydream about Noah's flood, imagining myself to have been one of Noah's daughters-in-law with a secure future, but in my more adventurous days, I longed to see the Republican River flood. Those who lived through it assure me that I was lucky not to have been alive to witness it. Now, more than fifty years later, hands still shake and voices still quiver as people try to express what happened to them, what they saw and felt. Without question the flood, coming so swiftly and in the dead of night, was one of the worst disasters that the state of Nebraska had ever experienced. Ironically enough, this enormous deluge of water occurred during one of the worst droughts the Great Plains had ever known. But in the spring of 1935, "things had never looked so rosy," wrote Bernice Post of Naponee. "During May we had received wonderful rains, after the worst dirt storms our country had ever seen. The valley fairly blossomed with small grain, alfalfa, and corn."

The rains, although welcome, began to lead to floods along the river valley as the ground started to reach its saturation point. In Red Willow County to the west of us, the *Gazette* prematurely congratulated its readers for having just survived the worst flood in their history. All up and down the river, farmers were wary as they heard the flood stories and, in some cases, as they watched the river rise to cover their bottomland.

Memorial Day—May 31—was a beautiful day. All up and down the valley, folks gathered at cemeteries to pay their respects. To the east, a farm wife took advantage of the weather to plant her tomatoes. To the west, in Denver, the fast Burlington passenger train, the Aristocrat, left promptly on schedule, at 5 p.m., with some hundred passengers and fifteen to twenty crew. But as evening approached, the air grew unusually still. Slowly clouds began to gather in the sky and, as evening progressed, they became blacker and blacker until a deluge of rain began to fall on soil already drenched from previous rains. Still, the rain was welcome, as it normally is in farm country, and most folks went to bed at their habitual hour.

When the rain broke in northeastern Colorado, it came down in solid sheets, beating against windowpanes with the force of hailstones. At Wray, Colorado, the last stop before the Nebraska line, the Burlington put a motor car on the track ahead of the Aristocrat to investigate the roadbed, and the train pushed on. "Faces are pressed against windowpanes," wrote one of the passengers. "There are lakes of water forming on the outside; the ditches at the sides of the roadbed are carrying roaring streams. The black fury above us is rent from time to time with streaks of lightning, and the thunder becomes deafening to us."

Just west of Haigler, Nebraska, only a few miles from the Colorado and Kansas borders, Jack Miller was heading home to Benkelman in his large freight truck when the rain hit. It caught him far back in the hills, and it came down so fast that it actually "crowded the breathing elements out of the atmosphere" until the air became stifling. Jack crept along, crossing the highway bridge over the swollen Arickaree River that feeds into the Republican, but as he saw another roaring river ahead of him, he was afraid to go further. He set the brakes and prepared to wait for the water to recede.

Instead of receding, the water continued to rise. "I actually believe that it rose five inches in ten minutes," Jack said. It may have. Unofficial reports of the amount of rain that fell vary from four to twenty inches, but without doubt, the rain was an unusually heavy one. A man who had left a quart pail empty in his back yard in Benkelman found it full the next morning. Soon the water was shooting up through the floorboards of Jack's truck. When waves struck, the stream of water would shoot clear to the top of the cab. Then Jack felt the truck begin to move toward the river channel. He found a stick, fought his way to the back of the truck, and pushed away the debris that was edging the truck forward. Still the truck kept inching forward to the channel. As Jack worked, he looked up and saw the Burlington passenger train going east. "I could have walked almost as fast as it was going over the Arickaree bridge," he said. "A hand car with lights was a few yards ahead of it. Doors and windows were open and people were peering out watching the flood. As the heavy train passed over the bridge, it seemed to me I could see the track settling, and scarcely had the wheels of the last coach passed over the bridge before the water began surging over it in boundless torrents. There was enough water there to have submerged the entire train in ten minutes, had the bridge and track given way." Jack watched as the train moved slowly into the Haigler yard, stopped for a minute, backed up a few feet, and then returned to its snail-like movement down the track with the handcar still leading it.

The train and the storm moved eastward. Near the tiny town of Parks, Merle Standish was awakened about 2 a.m. by the roar of approaching floodwaters. He roused his family and the ranch hands, sent the men on horseback to cut the pasture fences and release the stock while he drove to a nearby ranch and put out a line call for help. Then he headed to a nearby lake and made off with a boat. On his way to Parks, he was met by the Burlington section crew that had towed the Aristocrat to Benkelman and by farmers answering the line call. About sixteen men — eight at each end of the boat — waded in water that was almost shoulder deep, fighting their way from home to home, rescuing family after family. They didn't get to the Archie Burke house in time. Near the creek, the Burke family had headed out on foot to try to reach higher ground. The couple and their two children made it to the filling station, but when Archie tried to reach the store beyond the station, the power of the waves was so great he was nearly swept from his feet. His four-year-old daughter, Lois, was swept from his grasp, recovered, swept from his grasp once more — over the creek bridge and down into a torrent of water. When the rescue crew got there, they found Archie wedged against the bridge with his legs and arms wrapped around the banister, and Mrs. Burke clinging to a gasoline pump near the filling station with one hand and fighting to save the baby with the other. The rescue crew took the Burkes and other Parks residents to the nearby Tom Ballard place on higher ground; more than two hundred people gathered there.

But bad as the flood on the north fork of the Republican River was, the worst was yet to come. For the cloudburst that had caused the Burlington to slow down at Wray, Colorado, also had hit further to the south, in Flagler and Seibert, near the head of the South Fork River, considered by some to be the most destructive river that enters Nebraska territory. The cloudburst at Flagler and Seibert was measured at eighteen to twenty inches, and it sent a flood tide moving through Cheyenne County, Kansas, to Nebraska at the rate of eight to nine miles an hour. The South Fork is considered a dangerous river because it averages a fall of seven feet to the mile through Kansas and, at some points, the fall is as steep as twelve feet to the mile. The flooded South Fork was terrific in both volume and power. "It rolled and tossed and roared and boiled," an eyewitness reported, each oncoming wave more vicious than the one that had just passed. It covered the river bottom with "plunging, rasping, weird, roaring, never-to-be forgotten cycloniclike speed." Near St. Francis, Kansas, the only town along the South Fork in that state, more than a dozen people were rescued from the lowlands by a diesel-powered tractor driven right into the water. Some of the waves crested over the top of the tractor but, since it had no electric wires in its motor, it continued to function. But not everyone was so lucky. At a shack near a filling station, Eli Courtright was wakened by the flood but barely had time to dress before the shack left its foundation, then collapsed. He waded, swam, and plunged for some distance before he was caught in a current and, after terrific effort, was carried near enough to the base of the hills so that he could walk. He started back upstream when his brother, Chris, suddenly appeared from the torrents, directly in front of him. Chris, like Eli, had been asleep in the filling station near the shack with his son, Pete, fifteen. They had succeeded in battering a hole through the filling station wall; Pete wriggled through, but the hole was too small for Chris. He had begun to batter the wall again when the building collapsed, and he was thrown into the torrent. Pete was drowned.

About halfway between St. Francis and Benkelman, Mr. and Mrs. Harvey Barnhart were struggling to reach the barn when Mrs. Barnhart stepped into a hole created by the flood waters and sank before her husband could catch her. She drowned.

About six miles southwest of Benkelman, Tom Herring and Marion Hudson were "batching it" in Tom's place, which the flood waters earlier in the week had rendered pretty smelly. They were still up when the wall of water hit the house. They held the door of the room closed against the flood for a moment until they realized the pressure was too strong for them. Then they made a dash for the attic, lugging a sack of flour, a lantern, and some tobacco with them. The water followed them; they cut a hole in the attic roof and watched the other buildings on their farm take a hurried ride to the river channels and disappear.

Mike Allen, alone on his South Fork farm, had gone to bed when his horse stuck his head in the window and whinnied. Mike couldn't think what in the world the horse had in mind. Then he heard water splashing. He dashed out the back door, but when he opened it, water flowed onto the kitchen floor. He ran to the yard; by the time he let his stock out of the gate, the water was so high that the hogs were swimming. He waded — and floated — back to the house, grabbed a blanket, and headed up to the attic. He decided not to break the attic window unless the water got worse. A short time later, the house gave a slip and moved about three feet. Mike lunged through the window, got on top of the roof, and was about to dive off when a flash of lightning let him see what he was in for. Huge trees floated by the house, and several strong cattle were unsuccessfully trying to fight the current. The water action turned the critters head over heels. When Mike saw a section of the bridge come floating down, he figured that he'd make a try for it, if it came close enough to the house. It didn't.

Purl Newman and his family were awakened on his South

Fork ranch to find their home hemmed in by churning water. Purl decided to load his family into the wagon and get to higher ground before the road disappeared. He rounded up a team of mules and—with great difficulty—harnessed and hitched them. The powerful mules didn't much take to the idea of launching out into a sea ridden with trees and bridges, but once Purl got them started, they did all right. "The rising of waters, the roar of the thundering waves, trees being uprooted like weeds, buildings, livestock, and even people floating down the river painted a picture in our minds that was horrifying and so terribly depressing, and as the wall of water approached, it didn't seem that any living thing in its path could survive." Sometimes Purl and his team struck holes deep enough to submerge them, and sometimes they were struck by floating debris, but they kept on going.

About dawn on Friday, the storm and the flood were nearing Benkelman—where the north and the south forks of the Republican River join. Groups of people began to gather, at daylight, on the hilltops where the valley could be seen. The sight was appalling. The waters had left the riverbanks and were rapidly covering the territory on each side from bluff to bluff. The water was deep yellow, and it carried a most repulsive stench with it. "It writhed and twisted like a giant serpent," rising first above the foundation of buildings and then rapidly approaching the window sills. Horrified, people watched houses they knew to be occupied topple and disappear in the rushing giant waves. They watched as the largest trees in the valley were torn up by their roots. They watched as cattle and hogs tried to swim to higher ground. Waves dashed against each other and leapt skyward "like giant sea monsters, twisting and leaping and unfolding a panorama of death and destruction in their wake." Most awful was the realization, by those who stood watching from the hilltops, that they could do nothing to help those caught by the tide.

Among the people trapped in a house were Mr. and Mrs. James Robbin Pettit and their six children. As the waters began to rise, Heinie Frenzen and Arthur Shaver swam out to the

Pettit home and tried to get the folks to swim out, but the children — except for the oldest boy, Edward, eighteen — were too frightened, and Mr. Pettit didn't want to leave his family. So the two men swam back alone. When they reached ground, about twelve men had gathered there. As they discussed what to do, a three-foot rise in the crest of the flood struck the house. The eight bodies were brought to town the next morning.

Mr. and Mrs. Frank Ferguson, in their middle sixties, were luckier. They heard the flood only minutes before it struck their house, but in time for Mr. Ferguson to raise a window and the two of them to climb to the roof before the house collapsed. They had just about reached the chimney when it sank, dividing the roof in two. Mr. Ferguson tore enough shingles loose to give the pair a grip on the boards; then they settled down and hoped for the best. Their roof-raft proved seaworthy and held its place in the center of the channel. Early that morning, people watching the flood saw the pair coming downstream, moving very swiftly in the center of the current. They watched while the raft hit an island formed by the town trash having been dumped there for several years. The couple grabbed tree branches and crawled onto shore. They weren't the only ones on the island; there was a skunk, an opossum, and plenty of water snakes. Hundreds of them. Mr. Ferguson killed several of them to clear a spot for the couple to wait. Other snakes clung to trees and were entwined around the bushes. "A large bobcat came within six feet of us at one time, raised its right front paw much as does a cat watching for a mouse to come out of its hole," Mr. Ferguson said later. The bobcat stood and stared at them for a moment. "He seemed to be in a stupor." The couple waited it out all day Friday, and all that night; they were rescued on Saturday.

About the only house that was directly in the current south of Benkelman that stood was the old Brethower house where Mrs. Cordwell and her children lived. Spectators watched as the torrents of water ripped around the house which seemed to defy the raging water; it stood like a rock. Later, folks remembered that J. B. Brethower, who had built the house, had reinforced the basement walls by bolting the framework of the house to the concrete — protection against a flood that never struck while he lived there.

As the flood moved on down the river, the story of damage, of narrow escape or of failure to escape, was repeated over and over again. To make matters even worse, a tornado struck McCook during the storm. Between one and two thousand families were believed to be homeless because of the devastation. It was said that more water poured past McCook during the height of the flood than flows over Niagara after the spring freshets. In the lowlands near McCook, the water was thirty feet deep and more.

The Nebraska Public Light & Power plant at McCook was located in these lowlands. At 4 a.m. on May 31, one of the plant's engineers called Joe F. Ward, chief engineer, to say that the river in the lowlands had risen to within a foot of the fill on which the plant was built. Joe didn't appreciate getting up so early in the morning, but he got up, called other employees, and went to the plant. The water was rising rapidly. He contacted Burlington Railroad and asked them to deliver two gondola cars of sand.

By 5 a.m., the sand had arrived, and Joe had put twenty men to work sandbagging the plant, but before the dike of sand-filled bags could be built, the water rushed in. It covered the plant yard to the depth of about a foot. Joe had his men stack the sand bags at the doors of the plant, but the water began to seep in. It was impossible to keep it out. Once it got in, it went right down into the generator pits which were lower than the plant floor. By 11:30 that morning, there was nothing Joe could do but shut the plant down.

At least there seemed to be no further danger. The water covered the road reaching into McCook, but Joe figured it had reached its peak. It was running more slowly than before. He was confident that, within an hour or so, the water would begin to recede and he and his men could put the plant back into operation. About thirty minutes later, Joe heard a peculiar rumbling noise. It sounded vaguely like the insistent grumble of distant thunder. Joe looked out the window to see a solid wall of water, eight or ten feet high, rushing down upon them.

Outside the plant, two men were caught sitting on a gondola car. When they heard the flood's roar, they stood up, but before either could leave the car, the water had overturned it. Neither man was a swimmer. The two clung to the car, their heads barely above water, calling for help. A quick-thinking man in the plant picked up a garden hose, hurried to the roof, dropped the hose down to the car, and pulled each man up to safety.

Minutes later, the doors of the south engine plant gave way and ten feet of water swept into the room where most of the men were. Few swam, but all managed to scramble up through the penthouses onto the south engine roof. Joe and two other men in the north engine room clambered onto a diesel platform ten feet above the floor. Water was soon at their feet. Desperate, they climbed onto a crane and began trying to break their way through the asbestos roof. On the roof, a man heard them. Picking up a heavy piece of timber, he crashed it through the asbestos in the vicinity of the noise. The timber struck Joe on the forehead, stunning him. Had the two other men not supported him, he would have fallen into the water. Together they bound his wound, a severe gash, with a handkerchief and helped him onto the roof.

The safety of Joe and the men on the roof was precarious. As the flood level rose to eighteen feet, the plant began to crumble. Only four hundred feet away from them were high, dry banks, but who could reach them with eighteen-foot-deep water raging between the roof and dry land? On the shore, as some two thousand people gathered, a rescue attempt began. First, a heavy raft of timbers was launched, but the current kept forcing it against the bank until the raft was abandoned. Then, about noon, a rifle shot was heard. A man on the bank was aiming at an H-frame that carried electrical conductors from the plant to the bank. His first shot missed, but the second one connected. The bullet cut one of the wooden insulator pins and freed a wire. On the bank, the wire was connected to a strong rope; then the men on the roof pulled the rope over and stretched it tight

Paul Wilson dangles precariously over the flood-swollen river. He's pulling himself hand over hand on the rope, bringing a telephone and a line for a small cable car to help rescue the men trapped on the power plant roof. Courtesy Nebraska State Historical Society.

above the water. Over from the bank came Paul Wilson, hand by hand. He brought with him a telephone and one of two hand lines attached to a small cable car. With the hand lines, the men could pull the cable car back and forth from bank to roof; with the telephone, they could establish roof-to-shore communication. The noise from the flood was so severe it drowned out the loudest shout. Three men were brought to safety before the H-frame collapsed, breaking the rope and the connection to shore, and dumping Bob French, a plant employee, into the drink. Joe thought for sure he was a goner; who could survive the churning current? But Bob managed to swim to the bank where he was rescued by rope.

Unexpectedly, a section of the north engine room's wall collapsed. Joe and his men felt the roof give way beneath them. Hastily they scrambled to the lower, but still secure, roof of the south engine room. Their situation looked desperate. If the north engine room gave way entirely, the less sturdy south engine room, its walls already cracked in places, couldn't stand long. Moments later, their situation became worse. The black funnel-shaped cloud of a tornado was headed toward them. The sky became dark. Winds began to howl. The men fell silent. Joe began thinking of his wife and his two little daughters, Janice, four, and Joan, six. Some men knelt and prayed. Then, several miles before it reached the plant, the tornado veered and headed off toward the west, but the winds became so intense that the men had to lie down and cling to the roof to keep from being flung into the water.

The flood reached its peak after the tornado passed. It began to recede, but still the plant walls crumbled. All during the long cold night, Joe could hear pieces of masonry breaking loose and splashing into the water. There was no food. Men shared cigarettes and took turns huddling in the shelter of the penthouse to get out of the wind. Nobody dared to go inside the penthouse for fear of snakes. Rattlesnakes. Scores of them had managed to ride the debris to the relative safety of the plant where they floated in through broken windows. The jostling waves had angered them so that whenever a dead or dying animal floated close by, they bared their fangs and struck at it. The men could hear the snakes, moving on the debris inside the penthouse, rattling and hissing. On the bank, men sat in cars with their headlights shining on the plant. After midnight, the waters fell rapidly. By dawn, boats were able to rescue Joe and his men from the still-intact south-engine-room roof.

The crest of the flood passed south of our town, Alma, a little before daylight. The full fury of the storm had spent itself; the wall of water was not quite as high as it had been at its peak. Most of the people in Alma were sleeping when the flood came by, but Mrs. Keester was not. She had awakened early when she heard the roar of the storm. By daybreak, she and her husband had already been down to the river to see if Mr. Keester's house was all right. When she woke Opal and Everett McKee, who were sleeping on the screened-in back porch, she was sure that the house, invisible through the trees, had been taken by the water, but it had not.

At home, my dad woke early, too. Before he had fully stirred, he could hear the insistent hum that was not consistent with his usual morning rising. For an instant, he thought himself back home on the farm hearing the familiar windmill's whirr. When he woke to how loud the noise was, he was per-

A front view of the collapsed Nebraska Light & Power Company building a few days after the flood. Lawn and driveway of the plant are now a deep lake. Courtesy Nebraska State Historical Society.

plexed. What was it, anyway, a freight train going through? Then why didn't it slow down? he wondered. But the noise didn't stop. By the time Dad got to the street, he could see glittering water at the edge of town. It looked like it was up past the Cudahy plant, up past the railroad tracks, maybe. "Zelma! Zelma!" He tried to rouse his late-sleeping wife. "Get up. There's been an awful flood south of town."

"Hoppy" Hopkins and his wife were already sitting down eating breakfast when they heard the noise like a freight train that wouldn't stop. They couldn't figure out what it was. Then the next-door neighbor, Mrs. Warren Fowler, came over. She said there'd been a flood and that the water was all the way up to the Cudahy plant. Hoppy said nothing until Mrs. Fowler had left. Then he told his wife, "That woman's crazy." There had never been a flood with water that high. After breakfast, the two of them went downtown to see how high the water actually was. When they found the flood three feet deep in the Cudahy plant, Hoppy had to revise his opinion. "That woman wasn't crazy after all," he said to his wife.

Had I been alive to see the flood, I'm sure I would have

gone—along with nearly everyone else in town—out to see the Martin Ekberg family rescued. The Ekbergs lived on a farm not far from town. They'd been warned of the flood, but Martin pooh-poohed his wife and daughter when they advocated leaving. "No use getting excited," he said. "I'll head the car out the gate. If the water gets up, we'll get out of here." But the water came up too fast for them to get out and, when their house cracked open, Mr. and Mrs. Ekberg, their daughter, Louise, and granddaughter, Bernice Lennemann, escaped to nearby trees.

The Ekbergs weren't far from the shore, but the current that separated them from dry land was exceptionally dangerous. The current came down along each side of the house and formed whirlpools at each corner. The problem would be one of navigation. Half the town came out to see the rescue. Genevieve Dugan, one of the people who was there, passed a truck on her way in. It had a dishpan covered with a cloth in back. "Bet someone brought her bread down to work it," she said to herself.

The first boats were too light and, even with a motor attached, could not make any headway against the swift current. Then Charlie Foster volunteered to supervise the building of a heavier boat. Charlie was an old river man. He had grown up on the Ohio River and learned to boat as a boy. By the time he was seventeen, he'd spent some time working on a river boat that ran between Pittsburgh and New Orleans. He'd come west to escape the river life.

Charlie's boat, which took a number of hours to build, proved to be navigable. Charlie and his fellow rescuers maneuvered so they slid in and rode that whirlpool, then slid in on the downstream side of the house and worked their way over to the trees. As the boat neared the tree, the improvised oar broke and they began to drift with the current. Luckily, they got to shore and got a second paddle. On the second try, they made it to the tree. Louise and Bernice were picked up first and landed safely a ways downstream. Then the boaters navigated the current a third time. As they brought Mr. and Mrs. Ekberg to safety, the corner of the house caved in.

The watchers, who had been engrossed by the spectacle,

slowly turned to go home. As Genevieve walked back past the truck, she saw the bread dough overflowing the dishpan, obviously forgotten.

Charlie and his crew went south of town to try to rescue the Bohling brothers, Albert and Irvin, caught up in trees near their pastureland where they'd gone to try to get their cattle to higher land. But the boat smashed up against some object in the flood waters and broke. Charlie and Otto managed to swim to shore where a second boat was being built. It held together long enough to rescue the Bohling boys.

Further east, along toward Naponee, Katie Drummond clung to the phone pole she'd climbed to watch her father, the hired man, and a team of white mules make their way back to the farm house they'd all abandoned when the warning about the wall of water came through. She watched the outfit make its way slowly to the house. Her dad, William Houtz, and George Stone loaded up a stove that William had wanted to get, turned, and started back. Suddenly she saw the wall of water. The hired man heard its roar. Katie watched as the outfit picked up its pace and headed back. "They'll never make it," Katie thought as she clung to her pole. But they did. The mules came on the run to get out of there. They had about fifteen minutes to spare.

Afterwards, when the water began to go back down, there was nothing to do but calculate the losses — of cattle and chickens, of family and friends, of houses, barns, and outbuildings. "There was nothing left of our place but a piece of well pipe sticking up out of the ground," said Katie. Other houses, like Mr. Keester's where the water was only six feet deep, were filled with mud. "I remember that mud," says Katie, "thick as mud pie but it wasn't like dirt and water mixed together. It was smelly, slimy slick stuff; you could slip and fall on it." Men and women cleaned out with shovels and remarked at the number of tourists the flood had brought to the river's edge. Hundreds of tourists came to the tiny town of Orleans; the restaurants and filling stations did a rush business. At Oxford, the number of people "dwarfed the Fall Festival" crowds.

The River Kitke-hahk-i

I was born and raised on the banks of an enchanted river, the River Kitke-hahk-i, named for the Pawnee Indians whose villages lined its banks long before my Anglo town ancestors, wearied of panning for gold in Wyoming, decided to make their way down its stream to search for a likely spot to homestead. The River flowed, as do most of the Great Plains rivers, from

Summer seems eternal on the River Kitke-hahk-i, where magic buffalo can still be found. Courtesy Nebraska State Historical Society.

west to east, reversing the daily path of the sun across the sky, originating in the Indian direction of Thunder Power and terminating, if such a word can be applied to water, in the place of Birth. Day and night the River flowed, without cease, passing placidly across the flood plains, overflowing its low banks in the spring, occasionally rising high enough to inundate dwellings in the south part of town but never rising high enough to threaten Main Street.

We didn't call the River the Kitke-hahk-i, of course; we called it the Republican. That was the English rendering of its Spanish name: *La Nacion de la Republica*. It was a Spanish joke. Kitke-hahk-i was the title of a local Pawnee tribe; loosely translated it meant "Republic" or "Republican," which struck the Spanish funny bone, such a name seeming much more appropriate to the colonists fighting Britain on the East Coast than to a bunch of savages. By calling the River "The Nation of the Republic," the Spaniards managed to slur the colonists and the Indians in a single breath. But despite its anglicized name, the River remained more Indian than European to me. That was part of its power to enchant.

By the side of the River grew the legendary Cottonwood Tree, sacred to the Teton Sioux, or Lakota, who believed the four cardinal directions to be east, west, sky, and earth. The cottonwood was the tree that linked earth and sky; it was the tree of the Lakota's dance of the sun. In reality, the cottonwood, a native of the plains, is as much weed as tree. A cousin of the mountain aspen, it has a short life span. Its serrated, heart-shaped leaves dangle like brittle bells from its upflung limbs and, when the moon rises full in the east so that moonlight and sunset strike the river tree simultaneously, the moon-silvered leaves jangle in the eyes like a troupe of dancing tambourines. Lying half asleep in the dead of a summer night, one can hear their metallic rustle: they leap to the slightest movement of the wind, rattling out a lyric peculiarly their own, a sound more haunting to the ear than the echo of golden bells ringing in the mind. The Lakota tied their sun dancers' rawhide thongs to the tall, straight cottonwood trunk, linking them symbolically, through the tree's root, to their physical mother earth and, through the branches, to their spiritual father sky. It must have been a gripping sight, watching the dancers mount the stiff trunk until they became tiny as ants, watching them leap and whirl through the sky, descending in bounds and twirls like the airborne cottonwood seed, dependent on the strength of the buffalo hide and their own endurance to bring them safely home again. The seed of the cottonwood is tiny and brown; it drops to the earth in a hairy tuft as delicate as a dandelion's head, as white as the cotton's pom-pom. Each spring, the trees along the River explode into a profusion of white, a June snow that covers the ground and takes weeks to melt as, slowly, the brown seeds take hold and a new stand of saplings begins.

The Lakota believed the cottonwood to be, metaphysically, the center of the universe. So did I. Literally. Growing up under the shade of the cottonwood, I never doubted for an instant that I was dead center in the middle of everything. Didn't the River that flowed from night into day run parallel not only to our Main Street but also to the Kansas state line seven miles south of our Nebraska town which, in turn, ran alongside the fortieth parallel which roughly splits the Great Plains into north and south? Three states below us — Kansas, Oklahoma, and Texas — lay the Gulf of Mexico, while three states above us spread out that even vaster waste, the gulf of Canada. And didn't our town, Alma, lie directly beneath the apex of the noon sun, on an east-west axis that a nearby nightclub immortalized by calling itself the Seventeen Thirty-Three? The club's managers boasted of being 1,733 miles due west of the Atlantic's rim, where New York and Washington hung precariously off the coast, dangling dangerously near Europe's edge, and 1,733 miles east of the serene but oddly oriental Pacific. If we weren't dead center, who was?

"The sun," insisted purists like my sixth-grade teacher, Mrs. Wilson, who argued that although my hometown might be in the center of the United States, our country was hardly the center of the universe. Technically, of course, I was forced to agree (who could argue with scientific proof in 1948?), but secretly I believed the purists to be suffering from a curious form of *Zeit-geist* centricity. They forgot that the late 1930s' world I was born into was a world narrowed by dust storms, bread lines, and Al Capone; they forgot that the world I grew up in, that strange universe of World War II, was an even more constricted place. Little lay beyond its borders but a sort of blurred polyglot holocaust. To the south hung the tropics, Pearl Harbor, a flash of red, and the strange Spanish breath. North of us was a British accent under a Jack London Eskimo land of snow and night without end. Like the Lakota, we greeted each dawn, but we watched with crescendoing horror as Europe struggled unsuccessfully to hold the Huns at bay; behind us, in the direction of Thunder Power, only Our Boys kept the world safe from "Japs" who seemed to clamber over the far horizon with faces like Kilroy. My Uncle Glen was the only touch of reality with that world. He was stationed in the Pacific, on Christmas Island, which still seems to bob on the edge of my mind like a brightly lit tree. He sent us grass skirts from Hawaii, but his world remained incomprehensible to me. We couldn't write to him, or send him Christmas cards, for fear we would give his position away. I never did understand why, only that "they" might find out. "Them." Those bad guys with their powder-blackened faces, the ones that hung out on the eastern and western edges of time.

Mrs. Wilson tried to discourage my narrow, antiquated, anthropocentric point of view. She coached me diligently in Columbus and taught me to trace Magellan's circumnavigation of the world on our school globe, that hard ball papered with flat maps stretched into unrecognizable shapes. "If you bore a hole straight down through the earth," she insisted, "you'll come out in China"—walking, presumably, upside down. I remained unconvinced. The universe of my senses stayed decidedly foursquare and flat, as flat as an Indian sand painting, as foursquare as our town, Alma, laid out along the line that ran between the two poles. That world made sense to me.

Sometimes, when my dad got tired of driving us down to Kansas to see if it was still there, we would stop instead at the bluffs just south of town and across the bridge, bluffs so high that the Republican unwound below like a ribbon laid across the fields. From the top of the bluff, I could see for miles before the horizon got blurry at the edge. Nothing hindered the eye, not even the water tower north of town which was the second tallest thing I'd ever seen. I stood atop the first and let my eyeballs stretch. To the north, the world seemed to fade away just beyond the Platte River, somewhere between Mari Sandoz's sandhills and Mount Rushmore, which Grandpa Kemper had seen when all four faces weren't yet carved. To the east, the world disappeared just about where the sun rose, somewhere, I calculated, round about Red Cloud, Willa Cather's Nebraska home, like mine, on Pawnee stomping ground. Mother had read nearly everything that Willa Cather wrote; she liked *My Antonia* the best. Below us, to the south, the world faded out just beyond the Kansas line into one vast plain of wheat. Somewhere down there, Judy Garland sang of rainbows and the Tin Man danced like a scarecrow on a pole. Somewhere down there lay paradise, which, according to local wags, was south of us a piece where it wasn't so damn cold in the wintertime. To the west lay Orleans, our big rival in basketball, and Stamford, seventeen miles away, where my father grew up. Beyond that, the world was one vast desert that stretched all the way to the Rocky Mountains, those ranchy Rockies with their payload of gamblers and prostitutes. Somewhere in between, in that mysterious upriver land, the sun set, going down, I always thought, in the middle of that imaginary line the government surveyors drew to keep the time zones apart, the line that separated real from western time.

I liked Mrs. Wilson, but she didn't seem to understand as much about the universe as our forefathers did, the ones who named a piece of land on the Massachusetts coast "World's End," and certainly not as much as the Otoe Indians who had given my universe its name. "Nebrath-ka," they called it, meaning "flat water." An appropriate name. Plains rivers rarely have the chance to tumble down cliffs or churn over rock; instead, they weave meandering paths across land that slopes so gently it seems level to the eye. Flattest of Nebraska's rivers is undoubtedly the Platte, which moves slowly across the floodplains, ox-bowing its way along, its several channels forming long braids, barely contained by sloping river bluffs so shallow in spots they hardly seem bluffs at all. From my higher perch south of town, I could watch the Republican meander, its waters running faster than the Platte but not as turbulently as the third major river in the state, the Niobrara, which churns down through the sand-hills across the northern extremity of the state.

A curious thing about the Republican is that no one seems to know exactly where it begins. Some say that it leaps fullblown out of the head of a Colorado spring. Others maintain that it is the legitimate child of two rivers, the Colorado's Arickaree and the North Fork. The sluggish Arickaree is a limpid stream more than a hundred miles long and twenty feet wide. It joins the shorter North Fork, only thirty miles long, near that tripoint area where Colorado, Kansas, and Nebraska meet. Still others argue that the Republican is truly formed only at that point where these two rivers meet the South Fork, coming up from Kansas, joining the others near the Nebraska town of Benkelman.

Determining where the Republican River ends is much easier; shortly east of Red Cloud the stream bends down and dips into Kansas, flowing south to Junction City where it meets the Smoky Hill River and the Kansas River officially begins. This Kansas River watershed drains the northern half of that state, its waters flowing into the Missouri and on down to the Gulf. In between the Colorado and the Kansas state lines, the Republican River arches up across southern Nebraska like the long slow stretch of a cat's back. A shallow stream for the most part, it spreads only a few hundred feet wide except at flood tide when it can become a raging torrent that spreads out for miles, contained only by bluffs such as the one I inspected the universe from. Depending on where you believe the Republican River begins, it measures 422, 445, or 550 miles long. Even discounting the Arickaree's considerable mileage, the Republican flows for quite a stretch: it is the 114th longest river in the world. Viewed from the top of my bluff, the River seemed to have no beginning and no end. It was difficult to consider it finite.

Even harder to fathom was Mrs. Wilson's contention that the world was round. After a close inspection of the way the horizon ran 360 degrees around, I was willing to admit that perhaps the world was circular rather than square, but flat it remained. Stare as I might, I simply could see no evidence that the horizon curved over at the edge, so the map of the universe in my mind remained as flat as a checkerboard. In its center sat our town, Alma, surrounded by square patches of green corn, yellow wheat, and brown plowed earth. The only untamed stretch of land around lay at my feet: the cottonwooded valley of the River, which was incised below the level of the plain. All the rest was checkerboard neat.

When my Anglo ancestors selected Alma's town site in 1870, the Republican River Valley still supported an abundance of wildlife. The valley was notorious for its bison. Buffalo Bill Cody called it the best game district in the United States; he bragged about the bison and about the size of the elk herd he'd

Main Street of Alma, Nebraska, my hometown, as it looked during my childhood. Courtesy Nebraska State Historical Society.

seen where Sappa Creek joins the Republican. The area was to
big-game hunting in the United States what Kenya is to Africa;
hunters showed up from all over the world to try their luck.
Even Duke Alexis and his men came over from Russia to hunt.
Guards had to be posted by the kill at night to keep the wolves
from the fresh meat — wolves, coyotes, and bob cats being as
plentiful as other animals. Although buffalo hunting had passed
its prime by the time the settlers came, they saw herds that
numbered in the thousands, herds so large that the animals took
several hours to lumber past any given spot. In the fall, when
the prairie chickens migrated, settlers saw flocks large enough to
darken the sky even though their numbers, too, had been reduced by the commercial hunters who trapped them by the hundreds to ship back East. Turkeys were less plentiful; as early as
1854, flocks had been wiped out by hunters raiding their roosts.
"Rattlesnake Pete," a former U.S. marshall, bragged about bag-
ging the last turkey in Nebraska, supposedly an old gobbler
roosting on a tree near the Platte. But catfish were plentiful in
the River, and mink, raccoon, badger, porcupine, and red fox
lived along the banks.

The cottonwood tree provided the early settlers with their
first boats. As Christian Rebman remembered it, "There was no
bridge, and it was hard to cross the River in the spring, so I cut
me down a cottonwood and made me a boat." The early boats
were dugouts, hollowed-out cottonwood trunks. "I could carry
two men across," Rebman bragged, "even in the spring current,
if I was careful not to tip." If he tipped, he and his passengers
could always swim out. The River was not terribly wide, and its
waters were slow moving, even during the spring flow, with
beaver dams dotted all across. The beavers were abundant — fat
and sassy and very large. One hunter, up by Orleans, boasted of
catching a specimen that weighed in at a hundred pounds.

By the time my parents were born, in the early 1900s, the
River had become quite civilized. Much of the wildlife was
gone, and bridges spanned the stream. The most famous were
the Twin Bridges between Alma and Orleans. Beneath them was
an island where folks went to picnic in the summer or, if the

winter were cold, as many were, to ice-skate. Early pictures show skaters silhouetted against the white ice down by the Old Mill, women in large dark flared gowns and men in narrow black pants. In May of 1904, the River's first steam yacht appeared. Her names was *Minnie B.*; she was twenty-four feet long, six feet wide, white, and anchored at the foot of Flag Creek. On her trial run, she set a new record for Republican River speed: one mile in four minutes.

For me, in the 1940s, the River was primarily an enchanted place. I loved to wander by its banks, watching overhead as the blackbirds ganged up on the sparrow hawk that swung lazily in an arc, looking for sparrows — or mice or fish. Sometimes the blackbirds would land, swaying like trapeze artists on the heads of long weed stems. There they would chirp and sway, sometimes rising on their toes to spread their black wings and give their bright red shoulders a stretch. The red shoulder patches were rimmed with gold; to watch a redwing blackbird swing was almost as exciting as catching a glimpse of the bright black and orange oriole climbing in a jagged circle through the trees into the sky. Sometimes a huge dragonfly would dart by low enough so I could catch a glimpse of the sun behind its wings, those iridescent net-veined wings more mysterious than those of angels stained in glass. Like all enchanted places, the River was not without its terrors. One went there at one's own risk, keeping a sharp eye out for sagging vines of poison ivy; fighting the air pools of mosquitoes that liked to gang up and attack humans en masse. Even the cottonwoods could not be trusted. The trees lived, died, and fell — at first into each others' arms, but finally to the ground, their crashes echoing in that silent place. One learned early to walk around those pairs that leaned against one another drunkenly, swaying in the wind. Who knew when, like the Saturday night crowd at the dance hall, one might not yield to gravity and come crashing down.

I spent a lot of time by the River's bank, sometimes skipping school to play in the woods. Despite its terrors, the River soothed my soul, but my sisters and I were not allowed to swim there. "Too dirty," my mother said, and perhaps she was right.

Certainly the River looked as muddy and brown as chocolate pudding. On lazy summer days when we'd tiptoe down to the River's murky edge and wade in, the water would be sluggish and warm. Squint as I might, I would see no signs of the typhoid fever germs or—worse yet—the polio germs that were rumored to lurk there, but the bottom of the River was clearly mud. Wading into it was like wading into pudding; the mud would surge up, thick and viscous, between my toes and dirt would swirl in patterns along my ankles not unlike those made by dropping cream into iced coffee—a swirling volcanic kind of cloud.

My father, like most farm boys, had learned to swim by that time-honored baptismal method called "sink or swim," a method that conjured up images of dead, bloated boys. Sometimes he would tease us by threatening to throw us off the bank and teach us to swim the way he'd learned. He swore by the method. "Never met a man who hadn't learned to swim the first time out," he chortled, threatening to throw us in like pups. Sometimes, when the water seemed cooler and more tempting than usual, I would berate myself for my own cowardice. Why didn't I just leap in and learn to swim, myself? On my brave days, I could almost feel my feet swelling into webs, but I could never quite imagine my face in that greenish-brown bath, so I would stop, hesitate, watch the river mud swirl up in volcanic patterns along my legs, and let my conservative mother win.

For River water was dirty, there was no getting around that. Even the fish we caught there looked dirty, especially the catfish and the bullheads. The scaley carp looked clean, but we knew better; we threw them back. "Garbage fish," folks called them, clucking their tongues at the way some people would eat anything. The carp were easy to catch. All you had to do was sit by the sewer outlet and throw a hook in. Sometimes we did it, just for sport, but mostly we fished for bullheads. They looked as though they'd been born in mud, their whiskered bull's heads melting into a scaleless brown body the consistency of a garden slug and the color of river-bottom mud when it curls and dries in the sun. The bullhead would come up out of the water gasping, its round eyes bulging out of either side of its flat mud-brown head, two spiny whiskers jutting out, forming a sort of Y. Bullheads make a whispering sound when they try to breathe air, and their wide, curved mouths smile even in death. My sister stuck her finger in a bullhead's mouth once. It was lying so still she thought it had expired, but River fish are tough. This one managed a last gasp and gripped the flesh of her finger with its tiny nubbed teeth. Her startled cry made my father laugh—my father, in his gray cotton fishing pants, standing at the gutting table, the knife cupped so easily in his brown hand that it seemed to have no more weight than a straw, its point slitting the creamy white belly of the fish as easily as custard, that creamy white belly that swells into yellow along each side. Watery guts spilled over the table as my father searched for roe, reaching his thick fingers in, breaking the ovarian sacs, and spilling the round eggs, shiny as vitamin pills, all over his hand.

The Republican was no exception in being dirty. All the plains rivers share that trait. They flow across earth, not rock, for the most part, and they take their share of silt on their journey to the Gulf. The Plains rivers are all that remain today of the great inland sea that once covered the land for miles around. Sometime before the time of the dinosaurs, the sea had dried up until only rivers remained, rivers and the tunnels of water that flow underground, all following the pattern of the land, which slopes slowly but steadily down from the Rockies to the Mississippi, that massive brown river which drops some 2,350 miles from its inception in Minnesota to its terminus in the Gulf of Mexico. At its point of origin, the Mississippi is so skinny you can jump across it, but soon that "long pliant apple-paring," as Mark Twain called it, spreads wide, running a mile and a half from bank to bank, tumbling along in a brown flood that discharges six thousand cubic miles of silt-filled water annually into the sea. That's about half the volume of the Great Lakes. The Mississippi drains, with its western arm—the Missouri River—the entire Great Plains; with its eastern arm—the Ohio—it drains a basin that runs all the way to the Appalachians. Small wonder the Indians called this river "father of waters." Each year Father Mississippi carries some 495 million tons of sediment off the continent, depositing it on a delta as large and triangular as that of the Nile, the gifts of silt accumulating rapidly enough to enlarge the delta six miles each century. First wife of the Mississippi has got to be Big Muddy, the rough and tumbling Missouri River, as flood-prone as the Nile but much less predictable. The turbulent flotsam-laden Missouri is the longest river in the United States, outstretching even Papa Mississippi by nearly 200 miles. Together the Missouri-Mississippi river system is the third longest in the world, its combined 3,710 miles outranked only by the Amazon's 4,000 and the Nile's 4,160. In Nebraska, the Platte River, forty miles to the north of us and the longest river in the state, was notorious for being a river of mud, particularly in the summertime when irrigation causes the water to recede to a trickle in the center of the flat riverbed, the wide bed itself reduced to flat crinkles of grayed mud that curled up toward the sun like bits of orange

The River Kitke-hahk-i was named for the Pawnee Indians whose villages long lined its banks. Here some Pawnee get ready for a scalp dance. Two scalps dangle high in the air. Courtesy Nebraska State Historical Society.

peel. The mud crumbled easily beneath bare feet, swirling dust up into the air.

Thanks to the plains water, which is not only dirty but hard, I met the Culligan Man, whose name sounded like Coke bubbling up inside a shaken bottle. His was a soft voice, less dramatic than the little pillbox-headed man who came crying into our house day and night: "Call for . . . Phillip Morris." Better still, the Culligan Man didn't stay inside the radio. Every once in a while he would show up at our door. "Culligan Man. It's the Culligan Man," sang out the voice in my head each time he appeared. The Culligan Man came to our house, my mother explained, not to doff his hat at her (which he did, invariably, even if only a touch of his fingertips to the pancake brim), but to deliver our supply of softener for the water, which we needed because plains water is hard as stone. Limestone. Which turns a sort of crumbly turquoise around the brackish brim that marks the water's edge at the spots where the River has backed down.

I loved the River south of town, but I wished it were as famous as the Platte, whose meandering waters had flowed counter to countless wagonloads of pioneers crossing the state. I wished its name were not a joke, but romantic, like Weeping Water in the eastern part of the state. Weeping Water was a translation of *L'Eau qui pleure*, so called by the French, a poetic people, who told a tale to match the name. In the early days, the story went, the Pawnee and the Lakota feuded over Niobrara, beautiful daughter of King Tatarrax, chief of the Pawnee Nation, whom a young Lakota warrior wanted to wed. The Pawnee, of course, refused and, one day, decided to ally themselves with the Otoes and go in battle against the Lakota. All was arranged, but as the warriors marched to the designated spot, they met — in the darkness of the October night — and each thought the other to be the enemy. They fought. When daybreak came, all lay dead, a discovery that caused the Pawnee and Otoe squaws to weep such copious tears that their grief formed a stream. They called it Ne-hawka, or Weeping Water. The legend, like many, has some basis in fact for in the River valleys of Nebraska, the Pawnee and the Lakota fought each other bitterly—although usually over hunting rights. The oldest settlements along the Republican, according to archeologists, belong to the Pawnee who built villages up and down its banks. In 1814, an estimated ten thousand Pawnee lived here, most of them concentrated in villages near Red Cloud and Hardy. By 1933, the Pawnee Nation had ceded to the United States all the land south of the Platte, land they believed no person could own, not even the white man. The Europeans drove them off the Republican and forced them into settlements along the Loup River, to the north and east, but the pull of the Republican was strong. As late as 1873, the Lakota surprised a bunch of Pawnee checking out the River way up by Culbertson, some seventy miles from where they were supposed to be, and killed eighty-six of them. Unlike the Pawnee, the Lakota were a migrant group; they roamed the western half of the state, following buffalo down from Canada and back. Mostly they fought with the Pawnee about buffalo rights, but they quarreled about turkey rights as well, turkey being a Lakota delicacy. By the 1870s, few Pawnee were left to fight. Most had been herded up from the River life and penned up in Oklahoma, on land so different from their own they must have felt perpetually adrift. By the 1870s, few Lakota were left to fight them. The bulk of the Lakota had been annihilated in 1869, pursued down the Platte River by General Carr from Fort McPherson, helped by Buffalo Bill and a regiment of Pawnee scouts. That left the valley open to the whites; by 1871, every creek along the Republican supported a settler or two. Like the Pawnee Indians before them, my white ancestors liked to snuggle up against the riverbank. In doing this, they were enacting a pattern as old as known human existence. As the foetus is said to repeat all the evolutionary patterns of its ancestors—from gilled fish through to human—so the settlement of the River repeated the ancient patterns of people everywhere who consistently choose first the river-bottom land. Rivers have formed the basis for settlement everywhere, in the United States as well as along the Tigris and Euphrates some eight thousand years ago. The River offers abundance, not only wildlife and game, but rich river-bottom land, re-enriched periodically by the floods that come down stream. But the River is a jealous giver; it exacts its price. The Egyptians learned to harness the flood tides of their predictable Nile, but the Chinese were not so fortunate in harnessing the much less predictable Hwang Ho, which, in addition to feeding the millions that called it home, also ate millions in flash floods that crashed down the river valleys in crests of fifteen to twenty feet. The Indians, before they left their River home, warned the early settlers of flood. They had seen, they said, the River flowing from bluff to bluff. The settlers, naturally, found this quite difficult to believe, that the River should swell, even with the spring run, from several hundred feet wide to three or four miles or more. So they ignored what the Indians said and, like people all over the world, snuggled into the River as close as they could.

My mother mourned the lot of the Indians. She thought they had led terribly tragic lives, being shot off their own land and herded into pens like cattle, only the pens larger, extending sometimes over acres of land. Worse yet, the government continued to cheat them every chance it could get, particularly when oil was struck in Oklahoma. Then the government explained to the Pawnee that, although it had given them the land, it hadn't given them the oil under the land. The same story is being repeated again today, only now it isn't oil on Indian land, it's uranium. Listening to my mother talk, I used to feel a sort of sorrow for this Indian land that was all but gone when I was born. Sometimes I would try to imagine how it had been when nothing but grass billowed under the wind, when everything looked the same as far as you could see. You could go stir crazy, the pioneers said, the way everything looked alike. Victoria Samuels, traveling by mule wagon in 1894, wrote of how she was warned not to stray from camp "'cause . . . you'll lose your bearings instanter, then walk around in a circle 'till you get a 'stroke' and die." Obviously, the prairie was a fierce land then, but it had a beauty as rich and deep as the Scottish heaths that my mother's people had long ago left behind them, miles and miles of green, wind-blown into a dozen subtle shades, fading into purple in the spring.

A herd of stampeding buffalo sounded like a wall of approaching thunder. The very earth seemed to tremble. Courtesy Nebraska State Historical Society.

Sometimes, in the River woods with the swarms of mosquitoes warring around my head, I could almost believe that those magical days were back again. I could imagine myself hunting the buffalo, tracking it for its power as well as for its meat. I would slide edgeways through the cottonwoods, waiting for the moment one of those shaggy, swollen goatfaces, all matted with brown hair but wiser than Pan, would come nibbling its way along the water's edge, grabbing up the saplings like blades of grass, eating with a shake of the head. I could believe myself to be one with those hunters of the buffalo who had lived here, in this place, long before I called it home. Sometimes I would imagine that I was Niobrara, daughter of that legendary Indian chief Tatarrax, a man whom historians say never was. But I seldom believed everything I heard in school. It was too easy to imagine being the Turk, that Indian who led the Spaniards to this spot, for the Spaniards — Francisco Vasquez Coronado and his conquistadors — were the first Europeans to set eyes on this place where I grew up. They were looking for the marvelous land of Quivara. As the legend goes, the Spaniards had acquired, in the course of their conquests, a Plains Indian slave whom they nicknamed "the Turk" in honor of his swarthy complexion. Through a translator, this Indian spun tales of his home on the shores of a great River six miles wide, full of fishes big as horses, and topped with dugout canoes that had golden eagles on their prows. The canoes were manned by rowers—twenty to a side—and some had sails. Under the greatest of the sails sat, or so the Spaniards imagined, the King of Quivara, Tatarrax, surrounded by his swarthy lords. Tatarrax worshipped icons that seem suspiciously Spanish—a cross of gold and a woman who was goddess of heaven. The Turk must have known his audience well. Every night, he said, this strange court was lulled to sleep by the music of a great tree: countless golden bells dangled from its branches to be blown incessantly by the Great Plains' ceaseless wind. Certainly the Turk's tale lulled the Spaniards. On April 23, 1541, they valiantly set out for Quivara, heading north out of the Rio Grande Valley, and traveling for some seventy-seven days on the high flat plains, notable, one wrote home, for its dearth of hills and for the odd humpbacked cows that grazed there. Buffalo, we call them, but they weren't those matted, moth-eaten specimens loitering bovinely in pens for the Eastern tourists to gawk at as they drive by. No, those buffalo were enchanted ones, great monsters who left their mark on the land in the form of buffalo wallows, huge dents in the ground where those shaggy creatures rolled around as gaily as a dog trying to rid itself of fleas. The wallows are scarcely visible now. Dust no longer flies there; pasture, or wheat fields, have covered the ground, but the dents remain.

When the Spaniards arrived at the fortieth degree of latitude—approximately the spot where Kansas and Nebraska meet—they found the River all right, but it wasn't running six miles wide. Not then. Which didn't mean that it never did. By the time I was born, the people in the Republican River Valley had come to know that what the Indians had spoken was true. On June 1, 1935, the normally placid Republican rose up as though in wrath. Heavy rainfalls at the tristate point, where the River begins, created a tumbling wall of water that rose six or eight feet into the air and spread as wide as the bluffs would allow, churning miles wide down the River floodplain floor and sweeping everything between the bluffs in its path. The flood struck with little warning; more than a hundred people died. The scientists called it a century flood, of the sort that happens only once every hundred years, but is responsible for carving the valley-bottom plains three or four — or even six — miles wide. In 1948, the River rose almost as high again, but the water came more placidly than before. Still, it covered farm houses south of town and came within a block of Main Street. The sun-sparkling water could be seen, even from our front yard in the north part of town. But the River the Spaniards found was a narrower one, dotted with Pawnee villages, none of which contained gold. Indeed, there was no metal at all except for a piece of copper worn by a Pawnee chief. The Spaniards were reluctant to believe this truth; they traveled some seventy-five miles along the riverbank, inspecting some twenty-five villages in all, continuing until they reached a place called Harahey where a Pawnee chief met the Spaniard's small band of conquistadors with two hundred warriors of his own. Here the Spaniards stopped and, after some heavy questioning, the Turk admitted that he'd led them on a wild goose chase. He had hoped, he said, to lead the gullible Spaniards off into the trackless plain where they all might perish and leave the Indians alone. But the soldiers had proved hardier than the Indian thought; instead of leading them to death, he led them home. "We strangled him that night so that he never waked up," recorded one of the Spanish soldiers who described the River valley as encompassing some of the best land he'd seen since he left Spain — flat, black earth watered with rivulets and springs. Nuts, plums, sweet grapes, mulberries, grass, wild flax, and sumac flourished there. Obviously, it had been a moist year. But in August, the Spaniards set out for Texas, wisely deciding not to face a winter on the plains.

Historians mock the story of the Turk; they say that the Spaniards never saw my universe. But I'm not convinced. Having grown up on the banks of the River, like the Pawnee, I can understand how the land itself can get under your skin. How easy it is to imagine that the Turk, taken to Arizona when he was still young, remembered only the great River that he once saw run from bluff to bluff. Certainly the wind that never stopped blowing was real enough, and as for the golden bells, well, cottonwood leaves are golden only in the autumn, but they do make magical music when their branches shake under the sun. As for his story about the wild goose chase, I suppose that could be true, but I believe the simpler truth to be that the Turk was homesick, that he had no choice but to bring the Spaniards here, to this spot where he'd been born. Better to die beneath a cottonwood tree than to be buried in foreign soil, however rich. I can almost see, in my mind's eye, the large circular earth lodges that he longed for. Perhaps their doors pointed, like those of the Lakota, to the east, toward the place of birth. How cool and moist those houses must have been in the hot dry summertime, and how the Turk must have longed for the sight of Indian women, bending over the rich River soil to care for the things of the earth: the corn, beans, pumpkins, squash, and melon that the Pawnee grew. The Turk's land has been buried now—ironically, by his own corn. It had been by the time I was old enough to see. But traces remain. Dents in the earth. Cottonwood trees whose silvery-green leaves shake like tambourines. Mulberries waiting to be plucked from the bush. There, south of the town where I grew up, on the banks of the great River Kitke-hahk-i that flows from west to east through the center of the universe, reversing the very path of the sun, traces of that place remain. There, beneath the upflung branches of the cottonwood that links true north and south, that links sky and earth, it is said— and I believe it to be true—the magic buffalo can still be found.

PART IV

Fire

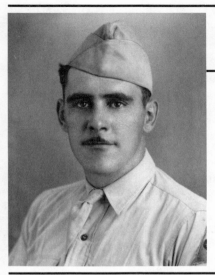

World War II

Some events are so overwhelming that they pervade an entire culture, touching the lives even of little girls raised in a cloistered environment, as I certainly was, growing up in the town of Alma, Nebraska, deep in the center of the Great Plains. Such an event was World War II. Too young to remember its beginning (I was only two when Germany invaded Poland), I had come into human consciousness by the time it ended. I was eight when the final armistice was signed. What passed as the official record of that war, the maps my father poured over and the news bulletins that the radio broadcast daily, largely passed me by. But the war itself did not. My earliest consciousness was colored by it.

My first war memory: I'm on my hands and knees in my mother's bedroom. Her polished wooden floor gleams like a mirror, perfectly shiny except for a series of black streaks that look like Japanese calligraphy against a wooden page. "You've

My quiet Uncle Lyle poses in his World War II service uniform.

been running in here again," my mother said when she saw them, recognizing that the black marks had been made by the sliding heels of my new shoes, heels made of synthetic rubber. Real rubber was no longer available for little girls' shoes; real rubber went into the war effort, as did silk and precious metals. My mother, the detective, was right. Against her explicit orders I had been running—and sliding—on the gleaming wooden floors, not expecting the very heels of my shoes to betray me. Now I'm on my hands and knees, eraser in hand, slowly, painstakingly erasing the long black scores until the wooden floor once again gleams clean, unmarked. I mourn for the days before the war, simpler days, when real rubber heels did not betray.

Scarcity marked the war years. I remember them by what we did not have. Butter. Life without butter must have seemed inconceivable to my father, raised as he had been on a farm where butter, like eggs, was a staple of life, but we—like thousands of other Americans—made the switch to oleomargarine. Oleo was white. "Close your eyes and you can't tell the difference," the advertisers bragged, but we could tell, especially in the morning on hot toast. Mother colored ours, releasing the little red-orange pellet that was packaged in cellophane in the oleo carton. The pellet melted and spread against the white oleo, its reds and oranges swirling against the white background like oil paintings spun at a carnival, until the swirls evened out to a consistent buttery yellow, only tiny golden streaks here and there revealing the imperfection of the coloring process.

The big buffet that occupied one wall of our dining room was the center of our war effort. Here, along with our silverware, were the Victory Bonds and the ration coupons. Each of us had Victory Bonds in her name, and we could open the shallow drawers, pull out the little booklets, and trace the patriotic markings ourselves. Tiring of that, we could look at our report cards from earlier school years or marvel at the velvet-lined case that held the silverware. The ration coupons determined mostly what kind of meat we ate, and how often. Too young to have to concern myself with the details of shopping, I no longer remember what the ration allotments were, but I remember suppers of chipped beef creamed over toast and dinners where hamburger patties were the staple of the meal. My memories of roast beef date, I'm sure, to later, more affluent postwar years.

Everything that happened happened in the context of the war. When my younger sister was born on January 7, 1942, we characterized the date as shortly after the bombing of Pearl Harbor.

The war was somewhat paradoxical: it was simultaneously far away, so far away that it hardly felt threatening, and close to home. My father had tried to join the army, but his business — he owned and operated a truck line in those days — was deemed crucial to the war effort, so he stayed home. So did his friend, Henry Stuhmer, who owned the local five-and-dime store. Henry, whose last name revealed his German origins, woke up one morning to find that his front porch had been painted yellow by some local who was unwilling to call him coward to his face. My father, too, must have experienced a certain amount of resentment over his exempt status. Fighting on the home front was not a popular stance in a war whose heroes were decked out in army drab. What a simple world I had awakened into! My earliest understanding was based on the deep paranoia that underlies wartime thinking: the world was split into "us" and "them." We were good and "they" were evil. The actual world was not quite this simple, however; we were of German extraction, too. My mother had been a Kemper before she married, and the Kempers traced their paternal line back through half-a-dozen or so generations to a small mining town in the mountains of Germany. My family never acknowledged this connection in those years. I was fully grown before I realized that I had a drop of German blood in me. For all intents and purposes, I was Irish — on my father's side — and English, through my mother's maternal line, the Johnsons. Discovering my German ancestry was a jolt that necessitated my rethinking these formative years, when to be German, or identified with the Germans in any way, was to acknowledge a connection with the Enemy, a connection that no one would care to make in the small homogeneous community that I called home. Had our last name been Kemper perhaps we, too, would have woken one morning to find our porch spattered with yellow paint. I've often wondered if my parents' knowledge of this was in part what sealed their friendship with the Stuhmers; there, but for the grace of marriage customs, we went—or could have gone. Still, it must have been an uneasy friendship to maintain during those war torn years.

The hysteria about the Germans was probably abetted by the fact that we had real live German prisoners of war incarcerated in our town. That they had been brought not only across the ocean but halfway across a continent to be imprisoned might seem strange unless one thinks of the Great Plains as the perfect place to detain foreign soldiers: how, after all, could they escape? Where would they escape to? The very vastness of the land they were imprisoned in mitigated against the thought, let alone the act, of trekking seventeen-hundred miles to the coast. How could they hide in such an open land? The prisoners were kept in an abandoned schoolhouse, a small square brick building where my mother had gone to high school, a building that had been abandoned when our fine new public school had been built. This prison was located right across the highway from our schoolhouse, and we were repeatedly warned to stay away from it. But my curiosity won out. I was not satisfied until, with friends, I had edged close enough to the old schoolhouse to actually see the prisoners. There they were, Germans, real Germans, their faces shadowy masks behind the window glass that contained them on the second floor. We could see that they were people, but they seemed more monstrous than human. We fled at the first sign of movement, as though they could walk through the brick walls that contained them and eat us alive. We fled, experiencing the thrill of having viewed the forbidden, a thrill similar to the one that could be had by going down to the Harlan County Courthouse and peering in the basement windows of the jail for a glimpse, if you were lucky, of a real live criminal who, at any instant, might peer out between bars at you.

Indeed, what a thrilling world I had awakened into, a world of heroes and enemies, a romantic world of conquer or be conquered that kept us all quivering on the edge of the chair. Adult life would seem tame by comparison. In a family where the father couldn't play the hero—what was heroic, after all, about running a truck line?—and where there were no brothers, the mantle of heroism fell on my uncles' shoulders, on two in particular: Lyle and Glen. These, my father's young brothers, wore the magical army uniform. I can see their faces still, handsome beneath their narrow rectangular army hats, Lyle with his dashing mustache and Glen with his wavy hair. Periodically these uncles of mine would show up in our living room dressed in their spiffy uniforms, their pants legs neatly creased, but they spent most of their time overseas, a place so far away that it boggled the imagination to consider it. Lyle, whose corporeal excess earned him the nickname of Tubby, was in the tank corp; Glen was fighting somewhere on a South Seas island whose name we couldn't know for fear we would inadvertently give it away to the Enemy, an enemy so devious that he might well have penetrated our little town which sat seventeen-hundred miles away from either coast. Lyle epitomized the warrior-hero for us. The tank corp with which he fought saw heavy action; during Lyle's stay in the war, he saw many of his buddies blown to bits. In my imagination, I saw him fighting on as tank after tank was blown out from under him, like some medieval hero losing his horse but continuing to battle on foot. Every once in a while, someone we knew would go overseas and never come back. "Killed in action," the telegram would read, and maybe there would be nothing to send back. This news would make a cold shudder go down my spine. What did it mean, to die? Once this news came back about Duane Cary, brother of Don Cary who worked for Dad. Don and Helen, his wife, were as familiar to us as my uncles. They and their parents bought, as a memorial to Duane, a large picture of Christ praying in Gethsemane, and hung it in the Alma Methodist Church where we all attended. I could never see it without thinking of this mystery, death, and why it hit Duane but not Glen or Lyle. We were lucky, or so we said. "Lucky Strike Means Fine Tobacco." What was luck, anyway?

Lyle never talked much about his wartime experiences, the family story went, unless he was drunk. Apparently, getting Tub drunk was not that easy. At least one story tells of him going into a local bar when it opened, ordering a drink, tucking it down, ordering another one, and so on. When it came time for the local bartender's lunch break, the bartender stayed on — thinking that surely this soldier would have his fill of liquor soon. But Tub remained, resolutely drinking into the dead of afternoon. He never spoke, the bartender said, and when he got off the barstool, he didn't even reel but walked out into the somber afternoon as though he hadn't been swilling drinks down all day. Tub wasn't much for speaking, in any case, but he had a hearty grin, and my older sister and I loved him as much for the hero he had been as for anything else, I suppose. Glen was as loquacious as Lyle was quiet. Glen was into kidding and teasing us; he knew how to come down to our level somehow. My sister and I were both madly smitten by him, and happy to crawl into the grass skirts and leis he brought back from the island with him, happy to show him that we knew how to hula with the best of them, even if we had been brought up in a backwater town. In a world where the best of men were heroes, marching off to war in faraway lands, it was easy for girls to be Guinevères, waving hankies good-bye, bravely holding tears back in order to cheer the men on. It was a role we were eager to play with our uncles since it involved flirting with them and teasing them while they were home on leave. We became expert coquettes.

In our rivalry for Glen's favors, we became aware that there were basically two kinds of women in the world: bad girls and good girls. Later, with increasing sophistication, we'd label them women who went all the way and those who didn't. Glen had at least two girl friends. One of them — let's call her Rhonda — was a city girl. He showed us pictures of her. She was very pretty, with her curled hair, and her lipsticked mouth, and her blood-

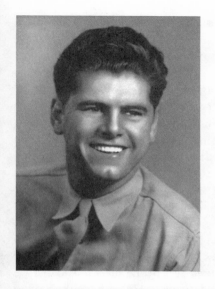

Handsome Uncle Glen, the heartbreaker, as he appeared during World War II. Courtesy Mary Coffey.

Me (in patriotic dress) and my sisters, Margaret (top right) and Margery (bottom).

red fingernails, but there was something vulgar about her, something that made us recognize a rival who would stop at nothing in her bid for his heart. Glen's other girl friend was Mary, a local farm girl, warm and generous and basically nice, though not as exciting, almost as forbidding as Rhonda. We felt sorry for Mary, sure that Rhonda with her red fingernails and her city-girl ways would win the competition for Glen. But Rhonda's wartime allure wilted with the armistice and, to our surprise, Glen chose Mary for his wife. We didn't know whether to be pleased or alarmed — pleased, for surely Mary in her infinite generosity would be willing to share Glen with us; or alarmed, because the allures of the world hadn't lived up to their reputation for power.

But in a world where males were largely absent, women learned to play another role, a role exemplified by Rosie the Riveter. I can still see her, on the cover of the sheet music that we bought to play, dressed in her fatigues, holding her riveting gun in hand like the machine gun it sounded like. Da-da-da-da. Rosie the Riveter. My introduction to the independent woman, the woman as hero in her own right, without a man. The impression that Rosie wrought on me, at the impressionable ages of six, seven, and eight, was one that I never forgot. Divine as it was to let teardrops hang on the fringe of the eyelash without dropping off, there was something gratifying, too, about building an airplane. Da-da-da-da. I could feel the vibrations running through my arms, jolting my shoulders, filling my body with a blessed fatigue that would cause me to collapse at the end of a double-shift day into a dreamless sleep that would allow me to rise, on the morrow, bright and fresh and ready to face the challenges of another hard workday.

For my birthday, my parents bought me a bicycle — a luxury item in those metal-short days — and I learned to ride. My father taught me. He balanced the bike for me and I pedaled away as he ran along my side. As I practiced, he held on less and less, until he was holding only the back of the seat, until he wasn't holding at all, and I was flying down the street, self-propelled, securely believing that he was beside me when he wasn't at all.

After I got over the shock of his betrayal, I had to admit that I'd ridden all alone. It was an achievement that I'm sure Rosie would have understood. Later, only weeks later, the paint on my brand-new bike began to peel. Slowly it lifted off of the cheap metal fenders, exposing the silvery metal until no paint was left at all, but I was proud of my bike just the same. It was a war bike. I'd had to sacrifice beauty for victory; it made me a patriot of sorts.

When the war was over, I celebrated our victory by marching solemnly around our block ringing mama's school bell. That we had any cause not to celebrate didn't occur to me until many years later, for I had incorporated the "good us–bad them" dichotomy thoroughly, and I celebrated our victory as purely as I would celebrate Alma's football victories in high school, as purely and as self-righteously. Not until I was older did I learn anything at all about the war itself, and particularly about the atom bomb. I discovered the atom bomb by reading John Hersey's *Hiroshima*, a thin volume that detailed the bomb's horrors in human terms. The image that epitomizes that book for me, the image that has remained with me through the years, is one of rescuers in a boat in the radiation-filled city reaching down to pull a survivor out of the water. Under the pressure of the rescuing grip, the flesh slipped off the survivor's bones like a glove off a hand. That such a thing had actually happened, that we were responsible for its happening—my revulsion knew no bounds. The "good us" picture began to show a few cracks. It deteriorated further at a church camp one summer when I met a German lad about my age. We became friendly and, out of curiosity, I asked him what the war had been like for him. Like me, he had been young, too young to fight even at the end. The thing that he remembered, he said, was his family piling its few household possessions into a wagon and fleeing the city as the Americans were coming in. He described his terror so graphically that it took a few minutes for me to realize that the Enemy, in his story, was my Uncle Lyle, coming into Germany with his tank, his Lucky Strikes, and his Hershey bars. That we could be the bad "them" was driven home to me suddenly as I stared at this boy, my friend, who had managed to escape being killed. What would it have been like for us if the Germans had come into Alma not as prisoners of war but as victors, their army boots pounding down our town streets? Would we have loaded up our car and fled, too? War was not as simple as it had seemed when I was a protected little girl, being raised—by an accident of genes or, so it seemed, by luck—in a portion of the world that had seen no bombs dropped, heard no machine-gun fire except in the movies. War was not as simple as make-believe, after all, and yet it had been. I was left with an aching kind of terror. What had I done to be so lucky, my German friend so unlucky? He had lost all of his family but his mother during those am-munition-ridden years. Nothing, I knew, was the answer, but if that were true then there was no guarantee that your side was the good side after all. Life was not as pure as make-believe either, and nothing I could do would return me to the simplicity and purity of those early years.

The Hoffa Years

One fine morning in September 1955, a three-hundred-pound man in a bright red Cadillac convertible was skimming his way south over the long straight flat-of-way that ran between Holdrege and Alma. He had passed the place where the hills turned into plateaus and was just about to the place where the land turned flat. On the seat beside him lay his shotgun, cleaned and primed and ready to go. He could have been a hunter, but he wasn't. He was Barney Baker; his profession: labor goon. He worked for the Teamsters' Union and that fine morning he was headed south, on the last leg of his 250-mile journey from

My dad, Tom Coffey, standing (at right) beside one of his early trucks. He gradually enlarged his one-truck company to a fleet of twenty-five trucks before he lost his business to the Teamsters.

A staircase conference between Jimmy Hoffa (right) and Barney Baker during the Senate rackets hearings of 1958. Courtesy UPI/Bettmann Newsphotos.

Omaha, to begin the process of organizing Coffey's Transfer Co., whose headquarters were in Alma. Alma! What kind of an outfit would headquarter in Alma, that two-bit town that lay alongside one of the two primary truck routes from Omaha to Denver, a town that sat and watched the rigs spin by, hoping to catch a half-dozen drivers for its diner, hoping to catch a dozer for its motel? Baker shifted in his seat and blinked; this flat land could lull a man to sleep, if he weren't quick. A two-bit outfit, that's what. Old Man Coffey had been working those drivers without a contract for the past five years. Time for such practices to stop.

Old Man Coffey was my father, and Baker was an emissary for Jimmy Hoffa, at that time head of the twelve-state Central States Conference on his way to the Teamsters' Union presidency. Hoffa had decided that the time was ripe for organizing the Nebraska carriers; he began by selecting key truck lines to unionize. My father's was one.

I, meanwhile, was a boy-struck freshman at Kearney State Teachers' College in my first year away from home. It was an outrageous year, in which I was accused of being a lesbian and during which I spent what seemed like hours on the floorboards of my friends' cars trying to escape from a passionate boyfriend who wouldn't take "no" for an answer. My primary concern that fall was my writing: I'd secretly gone to school to train myself to be a writer, an ambition so grandiose that I'd told no one about it except my closest friends. That September I was looking forward to the school's composition course and counting the number of boys in each class, figuring my odds.

I heard about Baker's trip to Alma from my father, who later wrote, "One morning I reached the office and found a fire-red Cadillac convertible parked on the street. A blubbery pug, weighing more than 300 pounds, was waiting inside. He said his name was Barney Baker, that he was in charge of Teamster organizing in the state, and then he *told* me, in rich Brooklynese, 'I'm holding a meeting of your men on the dock at ten a.m.'

"Ten o'clock was one of our busiest times, an hour when we'd be fighting to get out freight orders. 'Not on my time you're not holding any meetings,' I said. 'Why don't you just leave?'

"I took him by the arm and though I'm six feet two and 225 pounds, I felt stunted alongside him. To my surprise, he left without a word of protest."

This trip of Baker's to my father's office in Alma was the beginning of a labor dispute that would ultimately change the whole shape of our family life. The Teamsters' Union's unfair labor practices came close to bankrupting my father's business, and drove him to despair. In an agonizing decision, he sold the truck line and we moved to Lincoln, the second-largest city in the state, where he began working as Nebraska's purchasing agent. I transferred from the small state teachers' college where I'd begun my college career to the mammoth University of Nebraska. My younger sister transferred from Alma's high school where a graduating class of twenty was considered good sized to the city high school in Lincoln. And my mother, who had been born and raised in Alma, left it for the first time. We became citified.

But at the time Baker drove his red car into our little town, we suspected nothing. My father had been in negotiations with the Teamsters' Union before. His truck line had been first organized in 1947 when he'd signed a three-year contract with the Teamsters. It was a special contract, without what my father called the "featherbedding clause," a provision whereby the drivers would be paid by the mile for driving and by the hour for unloading, allowing them—or so my father said—to featherbed on the dock. When this contract ran out, the Teamsters had insisted that my father sign the regular Central States contract, with the featherbedding clause, or get ready for a strike. Dad had responded by sending back his drivers' union cards; then he hunkered in and waited for the strike. It never came. "Hoffa was too busy for small potatoes," my dad heard, via the grapevine. Hoffa remained too busy for five more years.

At Kearney State, my classes were going well, except for biology—zoology, actually. There was so much material to cover in the course, the material was so difficult. Dr. Bluse (pronounced "blue-say") was a demanding instructor and, much to my humiliation, I had broken a glass slide in lab right after Dr. Bluse had told us all a story about the stupid freshman in his last-year's class who kept breaking the slides. Leota, my roommate, and I had elaborate plans for decorating the small room we shared in Case Hall, the girls' dormitory, and I was sitting beside a cute guy in speech class. Barney Baker was no one to me.

The morning of September 22, 1955, three of the seven men who worked for my father in his Omaha office went on strike. They picketed. My father immediately fired them, hired three new men, and kept his trucks rolling. His offices at Alma, Holdrege, and Lincoln had no pickets; only the Omaha office was having trouble. Within three days, the trouble increased. "Imported labor goons appeared," my father told me, "and began their campaign of harassment, obviously intended to scare us into signing their contract." Six, and sometimes eight, of these men sat in cars parked around the Omaha terminal, often blocking the driveway. "In full view of the passing traffic they would clean their shotguns," my father said. "When they were questioned, they said it was hunting season and they were getting ready to do some shooting. If one of our trucks pulled away, they'd follow. If it stopped to pick up or unload freight, they would picket the terminal. None of this did our business any good."

My father's business was a small one. He had twenty-five bright red Coffey's Transfer trucks that ran from Omaha to Denver, drop-shipping goods to some ninety Nebraska and Kansas towns along the way. His payroll supported some thirty-five families; in Alma, alone, that payroll was $100,000. In opposition to this business was the national Teamsters' Union, a mammoth operation with $36 million in its strike fund. "We're waging a clean fight," Baker, head of the crew of labor goons, told the newspapers.

The second week, the fight escalated. Violence began. Ice picks punctured truck tires. Wiring was torn out of motors. Air hoses were stuffed with wadded paper so the brakes would fail. Drivers' wives received threatening phone calls. Callers said things like, "If you want your Johnny to get home from that junior high school at three-thirty today, you better tell your old man to stop driving for Coffey." My dad got calls in the middle of the night, calls that he picked up on his bedside phone. "Hello," he would say, but there would be no answer. Then he'd lie awake and wonder just how bad it would get. Fires and dynamiting marked labor disputes in Texas. A trucker was shot at twenty times in Tennessee. In Ohio, a terminal had been raided and some $4 thousand worth of truck tires slashed. Would it be like that here? It could be, he feared.

One weekend when I was home from school watching television with my folks and my little sister, something crashed against the front porch. It sounded like a rock — or maybe a bomb, my father thought. Before I knew what was happening, my father hit the lights and was herding us rapidly to the back of the house. He left; I saw the yard lights go on. We all waited. The sounds of the night reverberated in the stillness. Pretty soon Dad came sheepishly back and gave us the "all clear." "Probably just some kids being funny," he said, but I didn't rest as easily at home as I had.

At school, zoology continued to be troublesome. I had learned how to adjust the microscope without cracking the glass slide, but had done poorly on a snap quiz. My piano lessons were troublesome, too. The piano teacher was a perfectionist. Every time I made the slightest mistake, I had to stop and play the passage over again. But my social life was active. I was dating regularly, a fact that didn't make me popular with my roommate, who was too shy to go to social functions "stag." I decided, after all, to try out for the Wagoneers, the school's marching girls' band. Along with two hundred other hopefuls dressed in shorts, I was inspected. To my surprise, I was one of thirty-six young women taken in. Altogether, I felt encouraged by my progress.

My father, however, was discouraged by his. He had sent telegrams to the governor of Nebraska and the mayor of Omaha, demanding protection. This had resulted only in some publicity. He had asked his lawyer to petition for a National Labor Relations Board consent election, but the Teamsters had opposed it. They began legal delaying tactics. My father had his lawyer bring charges against the union before the NLRB, citing secondary boycott, a violation of the Taft-Hartley law. For the union had boycotted Dad's goods. A truck line that depends on drop shipping for its existence has to receive its goods from other, larger lines. Most of these lines refused to interline with Coffey's Transfer, despite the fact that some of them had shipped via Coffey's for twenty years or more. One trucker, Ralph Darling, who continued to ship goods with my father, was

Senator Tom Coffey, my dad, seated at his unicameral desk a few years prior to his tangle with Jimmy Hoffa, before his hair turned white overnight.

soon facing a shutdown of his own at his Kansas City terminal. My father began to lose sleep — and weight. Seemingly overnight, his hair, which had been flecked with gray, turned white.

Months edged by. Zoology yielded to my cramming. I got an A minus on the final exam and a B in the course. The piano teacher told me that my playing was basically good but needed polishing, a remark that I construed as a compliment, much to my delight. I was writing for the school paper, which gave me the chance to see my work in print. My roommate and I came to a rather bitter parting of the ways. She called me "odd," which didn't bother me since I was quite popular with both men and women. My new roommate, Beverly, and I were getting along fine. At home, my father was making the decision that would change our lives.

The decision — to sell the truck line — was not an easy one for my father to make. He was forty-nine years old, and he had been in trucking almost his entire life. He had become a trucker in March 1929, carting corn and livestock to market for his farmer neighbors in those deep depression years. But by the end of February, his cash was gone, his credit had been cut nearly in half, and so much bitterness had been stirred up that he seriously doubted that he could ever get back all of his old customers even should the strike be lifted. By the last week in February, Dad had made up his mind. He called together his men in the Alma office and told them, in a meeting notable for its silence, that he had decided to sell out.

When the news reached Kearney State's campus, I became something of a celebrity. Most people, particularly my teachers, were warm and sympathetic about the news, but one student in particular, a young man I had been dating fairly regularly, chose to treat me like a fallen social creature. I was astonished at the pleasure he seemed to take in my misfortune. Needless to say, we stopped dating, even though he eventually asked me out again a few weeks later when I had won a state championship in oratory and become something of a celebrity again, this time in my own right. The news that my father had decided to sell out came as a shock to me. I wrote my family asking for the financial ramifications of the act. Would I be able to continue school? I was relieved to find out that I would, but soon I was faced with a major decision. Did I want to continue school at Kearney State or did I want to move to Lincoln with my parents and attend Nebraska U?

The more I thought about it, the more a move to Lincoln seemed like a good idea. My first year of college had been a resounding success; everything I touched seemed to turn to gold. My grades were excellent and, in addition to winning the state oratory prize, I had won first prize in an essay contest for a short story I'd written. But scholastically, I was under pressure to major in education. Kearney was, after all, a state teachers' college, but I was far from certain I wanted to teach. The university would give me a wider range. But the turning point was my social life. Life in Case dormitory had become uncomfortable after I was accused — anonymously, of course — of being a lesbian. The accusation rested on a party a few of us had thrown, an innocent enough party that got slightly boisterous and spilled out into the hall. A few of us were wearing nothing but underpants and French berets. Word flashed around the dormitory that we were queer. The irony of the accusation wasn't lost on me. At that time, I was trying to dodge a boy friend who had become too possessive. I had decided to break up with him at about the same time he decided that he couldn't — and wouldn't — live without me. He used to hang around the dormitory entrance, waiting for me to leave for class so he could pursue me down the sidewalk, arguing with me. I was afraid of him. Primarily, I was afraid that he wouldn't let go and that I'd have to face the fall semester with this unwanted ex-boyfriend in tow. I think I was probably right about his tenacity, for when we moved to Lincoln, he found out where I lived, somehow, and one day showed up on my doorstep. In an unprecedented move, I appealed to my father to intervene. Generously, he did. I never knew what my father said to the young man; whatever he said worked. I never saw my ex-boyfriend again.

The Teamsters' Union receded somewhat in our lives after the move to Lincoln, but it did not disappear. My father was called upon to testify about his experience in the state senate, where he was booed when he said that he feared Jimmy Hoffa more than he feared Russia. But he did. By that time, he saw what was happening to him as a part of a much larger, and potentially dangerous, process. The Teamsters, in his view, were greedy for power. Hoffa would not be content with organizing the truck lines in Nebraska and the other midwestern states. He intended to organize every grocer, every merchant that the truck lines delivered to. My father knew, because Barney Baker had told him of the union's plans to organize every "nail peddler and prune pusher."

"How can you justify that?" Dad asked the organizer.

"Grocery carts have four wheels," Baker replied.

My transfer to the university changed many things. For one, I nearly flunked my second year of French, the university standards of accomplishment in the first year having been so much higher than those at Kearney State. I resolved to major in journalism. It was a compromise between the English that I loved and the education major that my parents kept threatening me with. I had to major in something practical, they insisted, so that I could earn my own living in case my husband died. I had all but chosen my future husband, an architecture student that I dated on a steady basis. Life seemed simple and clear.

Then, in November 1958, my father was summoned to Washington, D.C., to testify before the Senate's Select Committee on Improper Activities in the Labor or Management Field, called the Rackets Committee by the press. My uncle, Glen, manager of Coffey's Transfer's Omaha office, had been summoned, too. My father decided that the occasion was historic enough to warrant taking the entire family; I was instructed to skip school and come along, an instruction I hastened to obey. My professors excused me from classes, and one of them stipulated that I write about the hearings themselves, so I went to Washington resolved to be a reporter of what I saw. The trip provided me with my first glimpse of the East, that mythological region which faced the sea. I wrote: "The most startling difference between Nebr. & the eastern countries through which we have been traveling—Ohio, Pennsylvania, Maryland & the Virginias—is the tie with antiquity evident in these eastern states. Nebraska, in comparison, is the strappling young colt, just learning to settle into prescribed motions. Narrow streets, houses built more than a century ago, antiquated architecture, narrow houses—these certainly separate the aged from the youth. The East is more compact. Town runs into town into town."

In retrospect, I remember mostly the great turnpikes— Pennsylvania's turnpike in particular—and the awe they created in me. These were the first turnpikes I had ever seen: the interstate highways had yet to penetrate the Great Plains. These great streaming masses of concrete gave me some indication, as did nothing else, of the staggering population of the eastern states. For not only were these highways huge, they were as often as not full: hundreds of automobiles streaming in both directions. Sometimes, along the great divided highways, you couldn't see the automobiles in the opposite lane at all. And there was no such thing as getting stuck behind a slow-moving vehicle: these highways had more than one lane.

Nothing I'd ever seen prepared me for Washington. The mecca of the United States, I called it. Its white buildings and monumental statues seemed to invite worship. Compared with Washington, our state capitol in Lincoln, located as it was in one magnificent building, seemed puny. Government went on and on and on here. While we waited for the hearings, we went to see the usual tourist attractions. "This morning," I wrote, "we viewed Lincoln's death pillow in the house where he died and the theatre where he was shot. It was almost morbid—the way details of his death have been preserved. 'Lincoln, because of his height, lay diagonally across the bed.' "

From Lincoln's death bed, we went to Arlington Cemetery to see the changing of the guard at the Tomb of the Unknown Soldier. It reminded me of England, of Christopher and Alice viewing the guard change at Buckingham Palace. At the cemetery, we watched a military burial, "the bugler standing high on the hill above the grave, the soldiers with their rifles ready to salute—the solemn decor of the whole proceedings was in tune with what funerals or burials should be—dignified solemn affairs, a last salute to the dead—if they, indeed, should be at all." We saw the Marine memorial of the soldiers raising the flag at Iwo Jima; we saw Mt. Vernon and Alexandria. But none of it was as fascinating as the hearings.

In the corridor outside the hearing room, standing on the marble stairs, I met a famous man, Robert Kennedy, counsel for the committee. His shock of hair looked unruly, out of place for a man in his position! In the hearing room itself, which seemed carved out of a single piece of wood, sat Sen. John L. McClellan, chairman of the committee, and Sen. Carl Curtis, the man to whom my father had appealed for help. We heard testimony from Texas, testimony that made me realize how lucky we had been in the fight in Nebraska. We heard tales of rocks and bottles hurled at the windshields of oncoming trucks, of trucks set on fire, of dynamite bombings of terminals, and of planned murder, although Buck Owens, twenty-nine, a one-time Teamster organizer from Texas, said he drew the line at murder or hurting women and children. We listened to a Teamster official take the Fifth Amendment when asked about the bombings and other violence. He invoked the Fifth thirty-seven times in twenty-seven minutes.

Then my father testified. He read from his notes in a clear steady voice, detailing the now-familiar story. The committee was incensed. Why, members asked a representative of the National Labor Relations Board, did the NLRB delay so long? Why did it take the board three months to count seven votes? Legal delaying tactics, replied the NLRB spokesman. Specifically, two federal court restraining orders obtained by the Teamsters. "One man's red tape is another man's due process," said Frank Kleiler, executive secretary of the board. A Teamster official from Omaha was called in and questioned about my father's case. He took the Fifth Amendment forty-seven times. Out of these hearings came a recommendation to Congress to pass a bill outlawing secondary boycotts such as drove my father out of business.

Before we returned to Nebraska, my father took us all out to eat in an old established Washington restaurant. It was the fanciest place I had ever seen, located in a narrow building several stories high. We ascended to an upper floor via a tiny elevator and were greeted by a maitre d' who was formally dressed. Even the waiters had on suits with red jackets. Our table was not far from the grill where we could see cooks broiling steaks. To top off a very satisfactory meal, my sister ordered cherries jubilee, which arrived flaming at our table.

Jimmy Hoffa's Teamsters' Union not only drove my father out of business but, in doing so, unwittingly drove the family into life on a larger stage than we had known before. The move to Lincoln citified us, but the trip to Washington enlarged our vista even more. What had happened to my father was not simply a local matter, not simply a squabble between a union and a manager; it was a matter of national import. We were not alone in what had been to us a disaster.

Badlands Revisited

I still remember where I was when I heard that murderers Caril Anne Fugate and Charles Starkweather were "on the loose" in our town. It was one of those moments suspended permanently in time—like the day my father heard the news about Pearl Harbor on the car radio as he crossed a certain bridge south of town. Or the day FDR died. Or the day, a generation later, when I froze before a barroom TV set listening to details of a report that Kennedy had been shot. Talk about *news*.

Not that the local press hadn't covered Caril and Charlie. They had. I'd read all about the young couple—she fourteen years old, he nineteen. Belly down on our new rose-beige wall-

Caril Anne Fugate and Charlie Starkweather as they looked a few months before their murder spree. Courtesy Journal-Star Printing Co.

to-wall carpet, elbows grinding into the nylon tufts, I read how they were wanted for maybe killing Caril's mother, her stepfather, her little half sister. But what did that mean? Only another family squabble. Why just the week before, belly on the same carpet, eyes on the same daily, I'd read all about that nice Mr. Williams, a shoe repairman over in Beatrice, Nebraska, only forty miles south of our town. Mr. Williams shot his wife, two daughters and one son, killed them as they slept, then ran down the basement and blew his head off. With a 16-gauge shotgun. Who would have thought it. And I read, the same day, a report about that despondent housewife up in Hibbing, Minnesota, who killed herself and her three kids because she was going bananas. Small wonder. Hibbing—what can you do in a place like that except count stars of a clear night?

Granted, the circumstances of the Fugate-Starkweather killings were a bit bizarre. The body of Marion Bartlett, Caril's fifty-seven-year-old stepfather, was found wrapped in newspapers and stuffed in a chicken coop out behind the Bartlett's one-story house where Caril lived. He'd been shot and stabbed. The body of Caril's mother, Velda Bartlett, thirty-five, was wrapped in what looked like bedclothes and stashed in the outhouse. Shot and stabbed. The body of Caril's little half sister, Betty Jean, only two-and-a-half years old, reporters said, was found near Velda's, stuffed into a cardboard box. Betty Jean hadn't been shot. She'd been clubbed to death and her throat slashed— skull fractures and lacerations, the paper called it.

Weirder yet, Caril and Charlie had sat a strange sort of wake with the bodies, staying with them for at least two days. Maybe six. Warding off relatives who came to inquire, shooing away a lady who stopped to buy eggs, calling in sick to Watson Bros. trucking company for Mr. Bartlett so nobody would suspect.

Still, when you added the details up, what had Caril and Charlie done, really, but lopped off a few of her kin? Big deal.

How could I know that these family deaths were only the beginning of a chain of murders that would make Caril and Charlie a Legend in their own time? How could I foresee that a young movie producer, Terrence Malick, would fictionalize them sixteen years later in *Badlands*? That NBC-TV would feature Caril's prison life in an hour-long documentary that, in turn, would spawn a book, *Caril*, which draws heavily on this TV footage? Or that the *New York Daily News*, running a series about "liberated" women criminals, would bill Caril as a predecessor of a long line of female terrorists, the latest sensation being Patty Hearst?

Today, Caril and Charlie seem well on their way to becoming my generation's Bonnie and Clyde. Born on the heels of the depression, suckled on World War II, isolated and alienated without the words to express it, Caril and Charlie shared more with my generation than we, perhaps, were willing to admit. At that time, in 1958, in Lincoln, Nebraska, we were prone to magnify the differences. There seemed to be many.

For one thing, I was literate. A junior at the university, I was busy stuffing myself on Shakespeare and the classics, and squabbling with my parents, who said classics wouldn't feed me. I should study teaching instead. Or nursing. That way, when my husband died, I could support the kids. Caril, who wore her dark brown hair in a ponytail and fancied white baton boots, was still in high school. She was considered a spunky kid with a "certain elfish charm" who could pass for eighteen. Charlie was an out-and-out high school dropout with red hair, bandy legs, and bad eyesight. At five-foot-two, he stood an inch taller than Caril. He worked on a garbage route, shouting obscenities at people, telling old guys how to drive, and generally acting surly. "Nobody knowed better than to say nothin' to me when I was a-heavin' their goddam garbage," he wrote of himself later. Illiterate. As his writing showed.

Besides, I had taste. Caril and Charlie might settle for hamburgers and TV, but I went to see foreign films and ate in one of the town's foreign restaurants: a pizza parlor, the first I'd ever seen. I would never have shopped for Christmas presents in a filling station—which Caril and Charlie did. They favored a stuffed poodle. Charlie drove a souped-up '49 Ford with missing hubcaps and no radiator grill; he wore a black motorcycle jacket and black cowboy boots, cheap ones, several sizes too big. He stuffed the toes with paper. No, he didn't impress me. Just another greaser, the sort who edges his car ahead of yours at the stoplight, revs the motor, guns out on the yellow. Or hangs around the hamburger palaces, wisecracking, "Come to town to sell your chickens, lady?" whenever he spots a set of "country" license plates.

Charlie was nothing compared with my literate boyfriend, Gene, a university senior, majoring in architecture. When he couldn't beg his old man's Mercury, Gene drove a hearse with print curtains at the windows. Our favorite sport was cajoling a buddy into playing corpse, lying solemnly in casket position with a paper lily in his hands, so we could cruise the main drag, laugh at pedestrians' double takes when the "body" turned and winked at them.

Charlie got in trouble with the cops, letting underage Caril drive his car. But not us. We were too smart. We had our illegal beer busts down by the old creek bed, forged our IDs so we could spin down to Omaha and drink hard liquor like the grownups did, bought our Trojans in the corner drugstore, and made out like bandits on the back roads.

But then, what could you expect? Caril and Charlie lived in the seedy north part of town, Charlie in his rented room and Caril with her folks in that ramshackle white frame house of theirs. Gene and I lived on the right side of town, though my sector, south Lincoln, was so good my folks could even look down on Gene, whose mother, after all, rang a cash register in the supermarket and ran around with air force base people, and whose father, like Charlie's, was a carpenter. My family moved to south Lincoln after my father's small town–based trucking firm collapsed under the brunt of Jimmy Hoffa's illegal union-organizing activities. That period of ominous phone calls, tires punctured with ice picks, railroad spikes heaved from speeding cars, and strange men in out-of-state automobiles conspicuously cleaning their shotguns outside my father's office initiated me to violence. My uncle Glen, known as the hothead in a hotheaded family, kept a shotgun on the front seat of his car and a pistol in the glove compartment. He followed our trucks out of town, daring any Teamster thug to mess with *him*. When I was younger, Glen fought the Japanese and regaled me with stories of going to Ku Klux Klan meetings with my grandpa; all those white robes had scared the bejeebers out of him, Glen said. Not that Grandpa was racist; there weren't any blacks in the whole county. He and the Klan went after Catholics, instead.

A year older than Charlie, I considered myself much more sophisticated, despite my small-town upbringing. I snickered knowingly when the university's prize poet-professor, Karl Shapiro, characterized the state as a "cultural wasteland" and left his post shortly after. I snorted up my sleeve when I read in the *Lincoln Journal*, the week Caril and Charlie went on their rampage, that only eleven shotguns and five pistols were found in the university's whole dormitory system. Didn't I know better? Why, my boyfriend and his buddy could hustle up a better arsenal than that between them! So I wasn't particularly impressed when the county sheriff found Charlie's hot rod—and three more bodies—some sixteen miles south of town.

Two of the three new bodies were discovered at the base of the stairs in an abandoned storm cellar. That seemed fitting somehow. Storm cellars are common in Nebraska, dug to provide shelter from the tornado funnels that periodically pass too close by. My grandmother had one, a cave dug half underground with double wooden doors at the top, cool in the summer and warm in the winter, but my family sheltered in our basement. "Stand in the southwest corner with your back against the wall," my mother instructed us. "That way, if the house caves in, you won't get killed by falling debris." We huddled there more than once, staring at the wringer washing machine and the metal rinse tubs, waiting.

Caril and Charlie went to the abandoned storm cellar to get warm—it was January—when their car got stuck. They didn't stay long; the place spooked Charlie. "A hole in the ground, looks like a bomb shelter," he described it. Actually, the cellars more closely resemble the World War II munitions storage units near Hastings, Nebraska, half-buried Quonset huts mounded with dirt like freshly turned graves, camouflaged with grass so enemy pilots couldn't spot them. "They cast no shadows," my father told us. But bomb shelters were a topic of considerable import that January. Russia had recently launched two Sputniks, and we had yet to lift off our first spaceship from Cape Canaveral. For that matter, we had yet to launch our first ICBM. And, with SAC's national headquarters only sixty miles away, Lincoln was bound to get a lot of atomic fallout as Russian bombers came streaking over Alaska, past our DEW line.

But we Nebraskans were used to staring catastrophe in the face. One learns young on the plains to anticipate—and steel oneself—against imminent disaster, to understand the meaning of that soundless vacuum that signals the advance of a twister. The Great Plains is a biblical sort of land where blinding dust storms and plagues of locust are not unknown, where winds uproot trees no machine could budge. It's easy to believe in the possibility of the worst out here. My ancestors were not the only people to die from the droughts. To midwesterners, Grant Wood's *American Gothic* looks optimistic, everything so spanking clean, turned out so proper and in its place.

The third body was found in a small shack not far from Charlie's car, which was stuck in a farmer's driveway with six spare tires in the back. When Sheriff Merle Karnopp spotted blood nearby in the snow, he called in reinforcements: his men, some Lincoln cops, and state troopers. They closed in on the farmhouse with a bullhorn and tear gas, not to mention assorted firearms. Some thirty neighbors—townspeople from nearby Bennet, population 350, and farmers—gathered to watch the fun. Okay Charlie, we know you're in there; come on out with your hands up, the sheriff shouted over the bullhorn. We'll give you five minutes. And for five minutes, as if in silent prayer, everyone waited. Then they were off, heaving nine tear gas bombs into the house, running in—guns drawn, running back out again, eyes streaming, waiting until the tear gas cooled down enough for them to have a look around. They found an empty house. But the blood in the snow led to the outbuilding where they discovered the farmer, old August Meyer, seventy. He'd been blasted in the head with a .410 shotgun at close range. The first officer in the door nearly puked at the sight.

That's when the panic began.

August Meyer was an old friend of the Starkweather family; Charlie, his brothers, and his dad, Guy, had gone to the Meyer place many a time to hunt. "If Charlie'll kill an old friend like August, he'll turn on his own father," Guy Starkweather said, and he bolted his doors and windows against the return of his son.

He wasn't the only one to worry. The farm people south of Lincoln did, as well as those in the little town of Bennet. The two other victims had lived there: Carol King, sixteen, and her boyfriend, Robert Jensen, seventeen, president of the Bennet High School junior class and member of the football team. They'd gone out on a date the night before, cruising the back roads, I speculated, as Gene and I were wont to do: parking on the crest of a hill, cocking the rear-view mirror so we could spot the headlights of any would-be bushwhackers before they saw us, slumped in the front seat, jockeying positions to miss the gearshift. We kept a pistol ready in the glove compartment, just in case. No bushwhacker wandering down some lonely road looking for trouble was going to mess with *us*. If we'd been Carol King and Robert Jensen, Starkweather wouldn't have stood a chance. No, siree, we'd of blasted his head clean off — Gene's gun was a heavy German model.

Robert and Carol had stopped to give Charlie a helping hand with his stuck car — a custom on the plains where it's a long trek between filling stations or farmhouses. They got taken to the storm cellar for their trouble. Robert was shot six times — killed in self-defense, Charlie said; Carol, nearly naked, was not only shot but stripped and viciously raped. Officials never did say how, but we could speculate, we who had heard, by then, that somebody, Caril or Charlie, had rammed a shotgun repeatedly down the throat of Caril's little half sister, Betty Jean, until she choked. We could almost see Charlie ramming Carol with his .22, could almost hear him hollering (in all-American fashion) "Up yours!" as he pulled the trigger.

Radio stations began broadcasting descriptions of Caril, Charlie, and the stolen Jensen car, a dark blue 1950 sedan with twin aerials on the rear fender, license plate 2-8743. The car was assumed to be hidden south of town—or else speeding across the plains in some great getaway scene.

People who lived near Bennet packed their kin, if they could afford it, and fled to Lincoln for safety. Those who remained picked up their guns and posted themselves by their doors. "Gonna shoot first, ask questions later," one farmer said. The sheriff told folks to call their neighbors every half hour or so, make sure they were still alive, and many people called out-of-state relatives as well. Ma Bell made out all right—but then she usually does profit by war or disaster. Phone lines out of Bennet and nearby towns were jammed all afternoon and evening—a preview of the panic that would hit sections of Lincoln the next day.

Back at the university, few paid much attention to the Bennet tales. We were more concerned with finishing final exams or gabbing about the shooting that had taken place up Seward way, about twenty miles northwest. There James Hahn, a sophomore at Seward Concordia College (one of "our" kind), had plugged a bullet into the spinal column of freshman Donald Miller, paralyzing both his legs. A dormitory quarrel. Donald, presumably unable to sleep in the wee hours of the morning, went down the hall to Jim's room to protest the noise and got zapped. Nothing to get het up about, police explained. Just some guys "horsing around with a revolver."

Kids will be kids, after all.

I was running an errand at the university's School of Journalism when I heard that Caril and Charlie had doubled back into Lincoln, killed three more people, and were currently on the loose, possibly in my section of town. Now that was *news*. For they hadn't killed just anyone. They'd killed three of our kind, decent folk—the sort whose kids wear braces. That changed my whole perspective. I'd gone to the journalism school in defeat, to switch from my prestigious liberal arts major in English to something practical: news reporting. But what an auspicious beginning! With nine people dead, the story began to assume national proportions. Sure enough, even the *New York Times* found it fit to print. As a budding journalist, seeing Nebraska news in the *Times* shocked me almost as much as my later discovery that my father (my own father! that shattered my faith in appearances) was not above self-interest. "I'll never vote against the railroads just because I'm a trucker," I heard him promise as he campaigned for the state senate. But my check of his record there showed that he consistently voted against his business competitors. I should have known. Still, in many ways, I was as innocent as I'd been when, secretly reading comic books behind our overstuffed rocking chair, I accidentally overheard the news of FDR's death — or was it V-J day?

I was no longer so naive when I heard about John Kennedy. My boss and I had dived into a New York bar for a quickie lunch, heard the TV, and sat too paralyzed to do anything but gulp Bloody Marys. Afterwards, like true reporters, we limped drunkenly back to the office — Fairchild Publications — to call dinnerware and lamp manufacturers, ask them what effect Kennedy's death would have on business.

My boss, Patricia, was from Brownsville, Texas, and she had a theory about the Midwest. "It breeds a certain kind of people," she maintained. "The wild ones. The ones who look like airline pilots, who never fail to open doors for little old ladies, who greet one and all with that perpetual midwestern smile — and one day pick up a hatchet and slaughter dear old mom. Or grab a rifle and strafe Main Street." I knew what she meant. Hadn't my freshman roommate been friendly with that blond-haired chap in her town who walked out of the bank one day and began indiscriminately gunning people down? A reaction to restriction, Pat and I agreed. To the unrelenting demand for homogeneity. But in 1958, I didn't consider that a regional phenomenon.

I heard the news about Caril and Charlie, appropriately

enough, from the head of the journalism school, a tough-minded newswriter, a man who encouraged students to the kind of enterprise shown by an editor in Camden, New Jersey, covering the story of mass murderer Howard Unruh. The editor called Unruh up at home, before the cops had time to corner him, and asked, nonchalantly, how many people have you killed, Howard? Unruh, a World War II vet, had killed thirteen, setting a national record for mass murders, gunning his victims down randomly on the main street. Our J-school director, for all his toughness, was a warm, jolly sort of man. He would later deny me a recommendation when I wanted to leave Nebraska to look for my first job. It was nothing personal. Hadn't he, after all, recommended me highly for my Journalist of the Year award? It was economics. He wrested money for his department (which later won a Hearst award for excellence) from Nebraska's tight-fisted legislators by showing them what a high percentage of his graduating seniors stayed in the state for their first jobs — a telling argument in a state whose university graduates were known for their mass migrations. But I still judged by appearances, then, so I listened respectfully while the director read the news off an AP wire and warned me to be careful driving home.

Hearing the wire-service details, I felt a chill or premonition and left — cutting swiftly across the school's flat parking lot to jump in my mother's Chevy. Safe. So far. The school's tall carillon, dubbed the "Singing Silo" by students, interrupted its rendition of "Nellie Gray" to chime out the noon hour. I pulled off of campus, crossed the main drag of town, and drove past the state capitol building whose four-hundred-foot tower, skyscrapering up from a massive two-story base, dominates the flat prairie sky over Lincoln. The Capitol's circumcised globe blazes golden in the sun and — to the delight of university intellectuals familiar with Freud — is topped with The Sower, a statue of a farmer scattering his seed, heedless of biblical injunctions. Symbolically jerking off there, right in the middle of town. A much gentler seed than the spray of ammunition Charles Whitman would let fall from that three-hundred-foot University of Texas tower, shooting forty-six people, killing eighteen (including his wife and mother), and holding one hundred cops at bay. Six-foot-tall, blond and blue-eyed, crew-cut Whitman certainly could have passed for an airline pilot. Fortunately, Caril and Charlie didn't have to compete with his body count.

As I drove home, I listened to the radio repeat what I already knew: that Caril and Charlie had doubled back from the August Meyer farm into the south Lincoln section; that they had cruised the neighborhood (Charlie knew it well from his garbage run) and eventually slept there, undetected, even by the Skyline Dairy man; that they were let into the fashionable home of C. Lauer Ward by his unsuspecting housekeeper. She knew Charlie; he used to shovel their snow.

Mr. Ward was away working at one of his many jobs. (He was president of the Capital Bridge Company and the Capital Steel Company, which supplied raw material for the bridge company, and director of several of Lincoln's banks.) Caril and Charlie hung around quite a while, binding and gagging Clara Ward, his wife, and Lillian, the housekeeper, in one of the upstairs bedrooms. Both women were stabbed to death. Charlie said he had to kill them in self-defense when the maid came at him with a gun. Later he switched stories, saying Caril did it.

Charlie met Mr. Ward in the vestibule as he came home for supper. The industrialist never got his topcoat off. He got Charlie's customary greeting: a blast in the head. Shot three times and stabbed in the back, although Charlie later vigorously denied that he would stoop as low as stabbing. That was Caril's sport. Now both were loose, cruising around somewhere in Mr. Ward's big black 1956 Packard, license 2-17415. "License 2-17415." The radio broadcast it over and over again.

I made it home okay, parked Mom's Chevy in our double garage, and hotfooted into the house. I found my mother cowering in a corner of the dining room, our portable radio, its cord stretched taut, blaring beside her. If I hadn't known better, I might have thought she was listening to a tornado warning.

"Thank goodness you're back," she said. I didn't have to ask her if she'd heard. Danger gave us a sudden common bond, dissolving our differences.

We sat as far away as possible from the curtained windows, debating whether or not to draw the drapes. Mother was for drawing them so Caril and Charlie couldn't see us, trapped like flies in a spider web. I wanted to leave them open. True, that might give the couple a clear shot, but at least we could see them coming. A decided advantage, I argued. With the drapes drawn, the pair could be within pistol range before we knew anyone was there. Mother finally, reluctantly, agreed.

Together, we listened to the radio.

Caril and Charlie, charged with first-degree murder and described as "armed and dangerous," were presumed to be somewhere in town. State patrol cars, still combing the surrounding countryside, were ordered to converge on Lincoln. About forty or fifty sheriff's deputies, farmers, and state patrolmen searched for the Ward car, fewer than the seventy-five searchers in the Bennet area the night before, but their ranks would soon swell. Between one and two hundred National Guardsmen were called into active duty by Governor Victor Anderson. "All the experienced combat men we can get," the governor ordered. And the FBI got into the act, as well as volunteers, as the words "a killer is loose in the city" spread. Talk grew of forming vigilance committees, of making a house-to-house search, indeed, a closet-to-closet one. Soon a total of twelve hundred men were guarding us. And that wasn't counting individual householders who stood armed in their yards, protecting their loved ones against imminent massacre.

Radio station KFOR put up one hundred dollars' reward for information leading to the capture of the pair. So did the president of the United Garbage Association—good PR for his suddenly maligned profession. Lincoln's Mayor Bennett S. Martin offered five hundred, stating that he believed the killers were still in the city, that they were using our town as a base for their bloody deeds. Governor Anderson put up a thousand.

Downtown, the radio reported, some of Governor Anderson's newly summoned National Guardsmen were protecting the National Bank of Commerce, which Charlie was expected to rob. District court recessed early. Hotel business began to flourish as concerned employers booked rooms for their employees rather than have them venture home.

Sheriff Karnopp sent up an airplane to help search. Charlie, he thought, would probably "ditch the car and get another one in Lincoln. We have to find the car." The Lincoln Air Force Base volunteered its helicopters, and citizens were urged to report any sign of a black Packard, license 2-17415.

Around us, neighbors sat in paranoid vigils like our own, although we didn't find that out until afterward, when the fuss simmered down to a series of cocktail-party stories. Many folks left their garage doors open and the keys in their automobiles. That way, people reasoned, Caril and Charlie wouldn't need to come looking for anything. Large fast cars, preferably with full gas tanks, were considered the best insurance.

Some neighbors took more drastic action, like the woman who filled up all her big cooking pots with water and kept them bubbling on the stove. "I figured they'd come in the back door if they came at all," she explained, "because our kitchen is close to the garage. So I waited next to the stove. When they walked in, I was going to pick up a kettle and heave the boiling water all over them."

With her bare hands, no doubt.

My father called. He'd been trying and trying to reach us from the state capitol, where he worked as state purchasing agent, but he couldn't get through. The lines were too busy. We didn't know it yet, but the news of the Ward family deaths piled up the heaviest traffic on Lincoln telephone circuits since V-J day. My father said he was vaguely acquainted with the dead man, and wasn't it awful, and had we heard about the stab wounds, and Vic (my father loved being on a first-name basis with the governor) might have been the last person to see Mr. Ward alive. "Don't come home," my mother begged him. He said he didn't plan to.

The stab wounds were quite a scandal. Not Mr. Ward's, but

the women's. And not so much the number, although there were plenty, but the kind. The media declined to report exactly on the matter—like Carol King's molestation, it was too awful to detail—but gossips said the work was clearly that of a sex fiend. The murder spree began to foreshadow that of Dallas-bred Richard Speck, who would brutally stab eight nurses in Chicago in a series of overtly sexual murders, and who would spend twenty to twenty-five minutes puncturing each woman's body.

But why? we wondered. What would make anyone want to do something like *that* to decent folk like us?

The radio kept broadcasting the Ward license plate number until we had it memorized. The station received dozens of phone calls—it would receive hundreds—describing a black Packard cruising someone's neighborhood. People were urged to stay off the streets, especially in south Lincoln. My mother began worrying whether my sister, Margery, would survive. She was due to be bused home from high school, to be driven right through the main target area. Should one of us try to meet her? Or was the risk too high? The warnings to remain indoors weighed heavily, but I volunteered, being young enough to enjoy the surge of adrenaline that anticipated danger provides. A rush, we'd call it now.

As I headed toward the front door, the radio broadcast another sighting of a black Packard, this one with three numbers of its license verified. The car was only blocks away. I hesitated. My mother urged me to stay in and let Margery take her chances. We listened while the station verified one more number on the plate; the car was a block closer to our home.

Speeding, I dashed to our tall hedgerow, concealing myself as best I could from the lethal street. Periodically, I poked my head out of the greenery to scan the block. How I wished Dad hadn't sold his hunting guns! I could use one now. Not for nothing had I dropped by the ROTC building once a week for target practice, strapping myself into a shooting harness, flopping down on my belly military fashion, sighting down the long barrel. I had a credible record for bull's-eyes. It was ironic that I should wait unarmed.

Margery, I had decided, would have to come the first most dangerous, half-block by herself. If she made it to the corner, I would signal her home by waving my arms. If it worked. Knowing the depth of Margery's stubborn nature, I thought she'd be as likely to slow down as speed up if she saw I was in a hurry. But I underestimated her terror: she came running. Not that it mattered much. By the time we were safely indoors, the radio had reported that the sighting of the Ward car was a false alarm.

With three of us waiting, things seemed cozier. Even so, we froze when the doorbell rang. Margery and I began a whispered debate about whether or not to tiptoe to a side window and peer out past the curtain to see who it was.

"If we don't move, maybe they'll go away," Margery hissed.

"But the car's in the garage, they'll know someone's home," I countered.

My mother, never good in emergencies, roused herself long enough to order us to stay put, but I argued against it. Wouldn't we be in a better position to defend ourselves if we found out who it was? Then, if necessary, we could call Father at the state capitol building and he could summon the National Guard.

At length, I tiptoed to the window, eased the curtain aside (I can still see that curtain, a sort of silky pink material with gold threads running through it) to see my strapping boyfriend, Gene, with his best buddy. Husky prairie boys both waiting on our front porch, rifles slung over their shoulders.

Naturally, I opened the door.

"Are you okay?" The question was automatic. Strange, how we all assumed Caril and Charlie wanted *us* or, if not us, then our best beloved.

We were fine. Gene and his sidekick filed into the living room to show off their firearms. They had loaded rifles; shotguns waited in the car. And pistols. Gene's buddy had a pistol concealed, strapped in a holster to his sturdy chest. His pockets bulged with shells. They'd volunteered to join Sheriff Karnopp, who had been broadcasting openly for a posse. The sheriff, Gene told me later, gathered every local lush from every bar in downtown Lincoln. Some had never held a gun before.

The sheriff armed them all; he had to. A weapon couldn't be bought in the whole city. You couldn't beg, borrow, or steal a gun, Gene said. Everyone had his hand on his.

And off the two bounty hunters sped, smelling strongly of beer and brandishing their loaded rifles. Let that smart-ass Starkweather try to get away from *them*. Fat chance. Old Charlie just didn't know what he was up against. Gene revved up the motor on his borrowed Mercury, waved a cheery good-bye, and peeled out.

Meanwhile, Caril and Charlie were hundreds of miles away, in Wyoming. They'd beat a fast retreat from Lincoln in Mr. Ward's Packard, heading northwest on Highway 2, one of the state's least frequently used roads. Just the route to pick if you need to evade the law. Charlie dyed his telltale red hair black with shoe polish, but he needn't have been so careful. The widely publicized state dragnet was actually concentrated almost entirely southeast of Lincoln. Officers had reasoned that Caril and Charlie would head down Kansas City way; wasn't K.C. the nearest metropolitan area that could afford them a hideout? But the two weren't thinking like 1920s' gangsters. They were headed for Washington state to stay with Charlie's brother, Leonard, a chef.

On their way, a few miles outside the small town of Douglas, the couple noticed a new Buick parked alongside the road. They pulled over to take a peek. Inside, Merle Collison, a shoe salesman from Great Falls, Montana, was stretched out, catching himself a little shut-eye. Charlie woke him with a bullet through the window. Merle staggered out of the car, was blasted back into the front seat — and eternity — with nine bullets from Charlie's gun. "People will remember that last shot," Charlie wrote of it later. "I hope they'll read my story. They'll know why then. They'll know that the salesman just happened to be there. I didn't put him there and he didn't know I was coming." Charlie could have been a Zen sage.

Then, of all the bum luck, the Buick's emergency brake

stuck. While Charlie struggled to free it, Joe Sprinkler stopped to lend a hand. He thought there'd been an accident. Here, help me unstick this thing, Charlie ordered, pointing his gun Joe's way. Joe spotted the body in the front seat and thought better of it, grabbed Charlie's rifle instead of the brake. As the two struggled, a Wyoming deputy sheriff, driving into Douglas on a routine errand, happened by. He didn't recognize the Ward car, but stopped when he saw two men fighting over a rifle. Caril hightailed it to his car, hollering, "Help! It's Starkweather! He's crazy, he just killed a man." And the chase was on.

Charlie dropped his gun, leaped into the Packard, and lit out. The deputy radioed ahead and Douglas cops set up a roadblock. Charlie tore through it at better than a hundred per, kept right on going. The sheriff and the police chief joined the chase—into Douglas's city limits, out again, guns flashing. Charlie stopped when a shot shattered his window. He staggered out of the Packard, hand over his ear, shouting, "I'm hit! You lousy bastards hit me!" A hollow accusation. Inspection showed he had a superficial cut from a piece of flying glass.

The murder spree was over.

Caril and Charlie were, of course, celebrities. Their doings were reported in some detail: Charlie ate heartily and slept well in the Douglas jail. Caril, "stunned and dazed," ate lightly, her matron said. That's because she had no idea her folks were dead. Caril, Charlie said, had no part in the killings. That's right, said Caril. She was just Charlie's hostage. Hostage, hell, replied Charlie. She had a gun; she could of escaped if she wanted to. He himself had no idea that the maid and Clara Ward were dead. He'd left Caril guarding them, he said, so she must have done it. Like she killed that King girl he'd left her to guard. Come to think of it, Caril was "the most trigger-happy person I ever seen." Hadn't she killed Collison? Oh, he'd fired the first couple shots, but that wasn't dead enough for her. She finished the salesman off. And hadn't she blabbered all across the state something about that the maid just wouldn't die? While he, by contrast, had wanted to give himself up right after the Jensen shooting, but Caril would say no. Sitting there in the front seat with a .410 on her lap. What's a fellow to do?

"She seemed to have a hold on him," Charlie's mother testified. Charlie wrote his folks: "but Dad I'm not real sorry for what I did cause for the first time me and Caril had more fun.
. . ."

They signed their own extradition papers and came on home — by car — to stand trial. They were afraid to fly.

Lincoln folks sighed in relief at their capture, even if we felt a bit foolish that they were caught in Wyoming and not in town. We stored our rifles away and let things drift back to normal — although nearly everyone found some excuse or other to drive out to the north section of town, take a gander at the Bartlett house, see where the bodies had been hid.

The Lincoln newspapers began running page-one stories about dogs. The *Journal* revealed how Charlie had brutally kicked the Ward's poodle, how their Chesapeake Bay retriever "may have been kicked once." The Humane Society looked for new owners: thirty people volunteered. The paper lauded them. Twenty more raised their hands. Photographs were published of the new owner and his daughter. A picture of Caril's dog, King, appeared. It didn't need a home, Caril's uncle was keeping it for her.

The newspaper editors, perhaps somewhat shamefaced for participating in a panic that had no basis in fact, began blasting the cops for not catching Charlie sooner. The December murder of a local filling station attendant — at that station where Charlie and Caril shopped for stuffed dogs — was blamed on Charlie. Why, asked editorials, hadn't he been caught then? The exposé of the police department was the biggest since Lincoln's great bank robbery of the 1930s, but nothing came of it. The cops, investigators decided, had done what they could do. They weren't to blame.

Caril and Charlie wrote pages and pages of confessions, especially Charlie: "Don't know why it was but being alone with her was like owning a little world all our own . . . lying there with our arms around each other and not talking much, just kind of tightening up and listening to the wind blow or looking at the same star and moving our hands over each other's faces. . . . We knowed that the world had give us to each other. We was goin' to make it leave us alone . . . if we'd been let a lone we wouldn't hurt nobody."

We read every word and speculated about their psychologies. We couldn't read enough. Charlie, we learned, was an artist. He painted, in oils, canvases executed in bold rough strokes—landscapes and animal skulls. The papers published shots of them. Once he painted an Indian—with red hair. "Like mine," his mother told reporters.

Charlie's IQ was measured at 86, four points below the normal range of 90 to 110. His vision tested at 20-200, a point away from being technically blind. Thick glasses corrected his sight to 20-30. "He may go blind within a year," his folks said, explaining his actions. They weren't sure why, but thought it was "some form of stigmatism."

But social stigmatism seemed Charlie's major problem. He was shy, with a "peculiar walk, as though he straddles a barrel," and he took a lot of razzing for it. Got himself into scraps.

"I forgot about my bowlegs," he wrote, "when me and Caril was having excitement. When I'd hold her in my arms and do the things we done together, I didn't think about being a red-headed peckerwood then."

Specialists were called in to explain him. "Socially," the university's criminologist said, "he was an empty man. The only way he could be important was by killing." But then, how to make a mark in a society whose people have been media-surfeited into indifference is a problem even presidential candidates must face.

Finally, nothing was left to say.

Second-semester classes ground on. I learned how to report news. In my senior year, I covered Caril's trial as part of a Journalism 171 assignment. "Nearly an hour before court opened yesterday afternoon," I wrote, "men and women jammed the anteroom. People pushed and shoved each other as they hurried down the hall. The uproar could be heard . . . from the courtroom." Still, the trial was lightly attended compared with America's first big murder scandal, over loaned money. In 1849, Dr. John Webster bashed in a lending doctor's head with a chunk of firewood, then dissected and burned the body. The Boston trial drew 60,000 people, some from as far away as New Orleans, so many people that spectators were limited to ten minutes each in the gallery.

Caril was found guilty of the murder of Robert Jensen and sent up for life. I went to Washington, D.C., to write up class reports of my father's testimony against Jimmy Hoffa's Teamsters' Union before Bobby Kennedy's Senate Rackets Committee. I shook Bobby's hand — he looked just like his pictures, only shorter. Still, it felt good to get back home — to civilization, "far from metropolitan gang wars," as one Nebraska reporter wrote.

In the spring of Charlie's trial, his story nearly got knocked off page one by the unprecedented news — who would believe it? — of a lurid "teenage romance triangle" that ended in death. It happened only some 120 miles away, over in Albion, a town about the size of Douglas. A seventeen-year-old high school junior killed his one-time girlfriend and her boyfriend on the afternoon of her boyfriend's graduation day — just before he was due to deliver his honorary speech. Chased them all around the neighborhood and shot them dead. What a pity! Such nice kids, too.

A year later, inside the Nebraska State Penitentiary, forty-three official witnesses watched Charlie get juiced. He went with his fists clenched, they said. A few hours earlier, when the Lions Club over in Beatrice (home of that nice Mr. Williams) asked Charlie to donate his eyes to an eye bank, he retorted, "Hell, no! No one did anything for me. Why in hell should I do anything for anyone else?"

Outside the pen's gate, dozens of teenagers gathered on the midnight of his execution. Most came dressed in blue jeans and bobby socks — the standard uniform. For them, for Caril and Charlie, for myself. Some drove in, car radios blaring rock 'n' roll; some made their pilgrimages on foot. One girl told reporters, "Some of us knew him. Some of us wanted to be with

him at the end." A repentance of sorts. After all, we didn't mean
him no harm when we called him a bowlegged, red-headed peckerwood. We was just teasing. It warn't our fault he took it all so
serious.

Charlie probably wouldn't have been impressed. "The more
I look at people," his confessions read, "the more I hated them
because I knowed they wasn't any place for me with the kind of
people I knowed. I used to wonder why they was here anyhow?
A bunch of goddamed sons of bitches looking for somebody to
make fun of . . . some poor fellow who ain't done nothin' but
feed chickens."

And he was silenced as permanently as we would have been
had we got on the wrong end of his gun. A penny-ante sort of
guy, thought he was such hot stuff, but what did he know? Of
course, what did any of us know then. We had only World War
II behind us, fought "over there" and for a reason; we didn't
have to watch napalm pictures on the evening news. We had
only six million dead in concentration camps plus who knows
how many in Hiroshima; we didn't have to witness Buddhist
monks going up in their own flames. We hadn't seen anything
yet. We hadn't seen Jack Ruby gun down Oswald live on TV. We
hadn't seen Martin Luther King toppled on his motel balcony, or
Bobby Kennedy's blood-stained head on the convention hall
floor. We hadn't seen Kent State. We had no way of anticipating
Juan Corona's hatchet killings of twenty-five migrant workers—
"the greatest mass murder in this country in this century," the
New York Times said (sounding like Ripley)—making Whitman's tower slaughter of eighteen look like small potatoes. Or
knowing we would watch Corona's record toppled only months
later by the unearthing in Texas of twenty-seven dead boys. We
had yet to shrug as cops cremated that SLA gang on the evening
news. Or to watch Terrence Malick's romanticized *Badlands*
flicker across the screen, making Charlie look like James Dean,
moving Caril to the right side of the tracks, where she takes
piano lessons, her hair gleaming like a Clairol ad, looking more

like the media stars they became than the murderers of ten, maybe eleven, people that they were. What did we know? After all, in 1959, Patty Hearst wasn't even six years old. Things were different then.

A Master Alumnus of the University of Nebraska-Lincoln, Marilyn Coffey holds an M.F.A. in creative writing from Brooklyn College and is an associate professor of English and Humanities at Pratt Institute in Brooklyn, New York. Her nonfiction, often about the Great Plains, has appeared in such publications as *Atlantic Monthly, Natural History*, and Associated Press Newsfeatures. Gloria Steinem hailed her first novel, *Marcella*, as "an important part of the truth telling by and for women." An interpretive reader/performer of her own work, Coffey has given readings throughout the United States, in person and on radio and television. She is currently at work on an historical novel, *Holy Rainbow*, set on the Missouri River in 1811.